WILD ABOUT
WARRIORS

WILD ABOUT
WARRIORS

Written by:
Fiona Macdonald
John Malam
Rupert Matthews

Miles Kelly

First published in 2019 by Miles Kelly Publishing Ltd
Harding's Barn, Bardfield End Green, Thaxted, Essex, CM6 3PX, UK

2 4 6 8 10 9 7 5 3 1

Publishing Director Belinda Gallagher
Creative Director Jo Cowan
Editorial Director Rosie Neave
Senior Editor Becky Miles
Cover Designer Simon Lee
Designers Michelle Cannatella, Simon Lee, Louisa Leitao
Image Manager Liberty Newton
Indexer Michelle Baker
Production Elizabeth Collins, Jennifer Brunwin-Jones
Reprographics Stephan Davis, Callum Ratcliffe-Bingham
Assets Lorraine King

Consultants Fiona Macdonald, Jeremy Smith, Philip Steele

ISBN 978-1-78617-831-2

Printed in China

British Library Cataloguing-in-Publication Data
A catalogue record for this book is available from the British Library

Made with paper from a sustainable forest

www.mileskelly.net

Contents

GLADIATORS

1 **Gladiators were made to fight to the death to please the crowd.** They fought in an arena (open space surrounded by tiered seats) and used lots of different swords, spears, knives and other weapons. Not every gladiatorial fight ended in death. Some gladiators were allowed to live if they fought bravely and with skill. Most fights took place in Rome, but cities throughout the Roman Empire had arenas for these events. The arenas were also used for wild animal hunts and for the execution of criminals. For the ancient Romans, violence and bloodshed were used as entertainment.

▶ A defeated gladiator appeals for mercy from the crowd by raising his left hand. The victorious fighter awaits the instruction to kill or spare his rival.

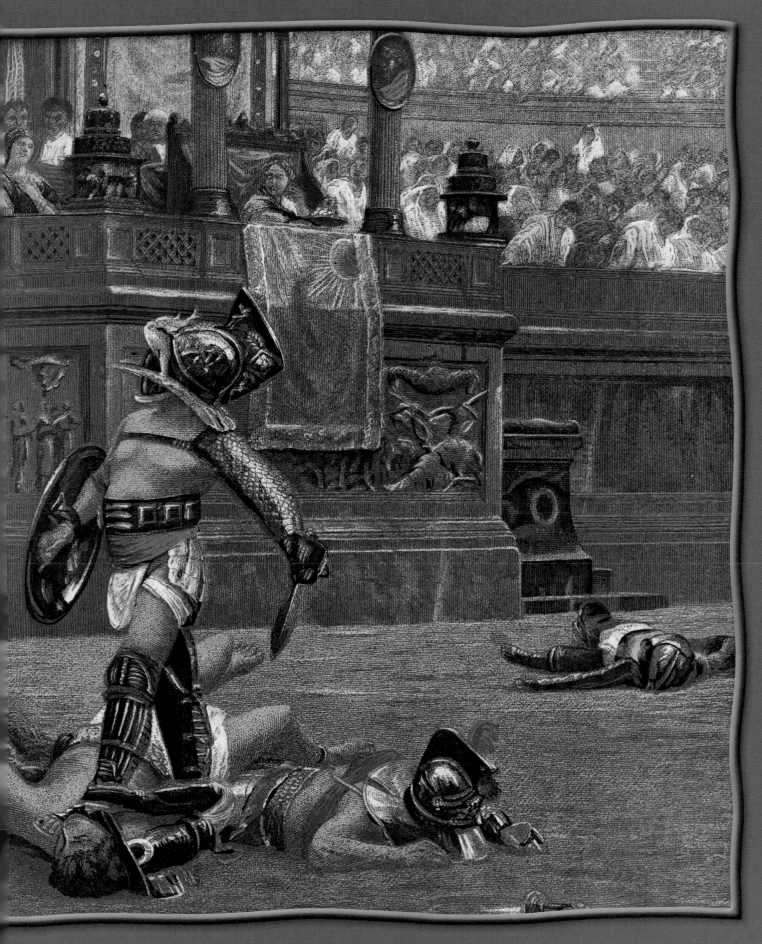

The first gladiators

2 **The first gladiators were not from Rome.** The Romans did not invent the idea of gladiators. The idea of men fighting in an arena probably came to Rome from the region of Etruria. But the first proper gladiators probably came from Campania, an area of Italy south of Rome.

▲ The first gladiators probably came from Campania, in the south, and fought more in this area than in Rome.

3 **The first Roman gladiators fought in 264 BC.** Six slaves were set to fight each other with swords, but they were not allowed to wear any armour. The fights did not last for long before one of the slaves in each pair was killed.

► The gladius was the standard weapon used by early gladiators. It was kept in a sheath called a scabbard.

4 **The first gladiatorial fights were always part of a funeral.** The name for a gladiatorial show, a munus, means a duty owed to the dead. The first fights were held at the funerals of politicians and noblemen, who ordered the games in their wills.

▶ The first gladiators were usually elderly slaves or troublemakers, who would not be missed by their owners.

5 **In early funeral games, food was more important than gladiators.** The Romans used funerals to show off how wealthy and important they were. Free food and drink were laid out at the funeral for any Roman citizen who wanted to come along. Gifts of money, jewellery and clothing were also handed out. The family of the person being buried would wear their finest clothes. The first gladiator fights were just one part of the whole funeral.

6 **Gladiators were named after their weapons.** The word gladiator means 'a man who uses a gladius'. The gladius was a type of short, stabbing sword that was used by Roman soldiers. It was about 40 centimetres long and had a very sharp point. It was generally used for slashing, not for cutting. Not all gladiators used the gladius, but the name was used for all fighters in the arena.

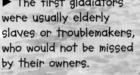

Scabbard

Gladius

Prisoners of war

▼ A Thracian armed with a square shield and curved sword fights a Samnite equipped with a larger shield and longer, straight sword.

Samnite

Thracian

7 Prisoners of war fought in the arena. Between 250 BC and 100 BC the Romans fought many wars against foreign enemies. Prisoners captured in these wars were sold as slaves in Rome. Captured soldiers were made to fight in the arena, with weapons and armour from their own country.

8 The Samnites had the best weapons. The Romans fought a long series of wars against the Samnites between 343 BC and 290 BC. These men each carried a large, oval shield and wore a helmet with cheek guards (flaps that protected their cheeks). Samnite gladiators were famous for the quality of their swords and spears.

9 The Thracians had the strangest weapons. The men from the kingdom of Thrace carried small shields and wore helmets with crests. They were famous for being able to hit any target with their spears and carried short, curved swords. This mix of weapons proved very popular and many gladiators adopted them. They became known as Thracian gladiators, even if they were not from Thrace.

▶ The tall, fair-skinned Celts decorated their bodies and shields with bright colours.

10 **Celts painted their bodies before going into battle.** The Celts were the only people to have captured Rome, in 390 BC. They lived in northern Italy and across Europe. The Romans forced many Celtic prisoners to fight in their native clothes and with native weapons.

◀ The Numidians from North Africa were famous for their skill on horseback. They often fought in the arena using light javelins.

11 **The Numidians fought on horseback.** Numidia was an area of northern Africa in what is now Algeria. The area was famous for breeding quality horses and its army included large numbers of cavalry (soldiers on horseback). Prisoners of war from Numidia rode horses when they appeared in the arena.

Gladiators and politics

▲ A person's ashes were stored in a pot or urn until the funeral.

12 Funerals were delayed for years. Gladiatorial shows were organized as part of the funerals of rich and powerful noblemen. However, the heir of the man who had died would want to hold the show when he was standing for election so that he could impress the voters.

13 A good gladiator show could win an election. In ancient Rome, votes were not cast in secret. Each voter had to give his name to an official called a censor and then declare how he was voting. The men standing for election stood near the censor to see how people voted. Putting on an impressive gladiator show could gain votes.

▼ A citizen waiting to vote at an election. The censor kept a list of everyone entitled to vote and people had to prove who they were before voting.

I DON'T BELIEVE IT!

In 165 BC, a play was interrupted when the entire audience left the theatre to watch a gladiatorial show. The actors were left alone in the theatre!

14 **Some politicians hired gangs of gladiators to beat up their opponents.** If a citizen could not be persuaded, by gladiator shows or the payment of money, to vote for a certain candidate, the candidate might use gladiators to bully him. Gladiators were armed with clubs and given the names of citizens who should be threatened. Every election was accompanied by this sort of violence.

▲ Men were posted at the entrance to the arena to ensure that only voters entered.

15 **Only voters could watch the games.** The purpose of holding spectacular gladiatorial shows was to influence voters. Only citizens of Rome could vote, so only they were allowed to attend the shows. Citizens who were known to be voting for an opponent were turned away, as were slaves and foreigners who could not vote.

16 **The best seats went to men who donated money to the election campaign.** Standing for an election cost a lot of money in ancient Rome. Rich men would give or lend money to the candidate they preferred. In return they would get the best seats in a gladiatorial show and would expect to receive titles or government money if their candidate won.

◄ Roman coins were made of gold, silver or bronze and carried a portrait of the emperor on one side.

Spartacus!

17 **The most famous gladiator of all was Spartacus.** He led a rebellion of gladiators and other slaves in the year 73 BC. At first Spartacus had just 70 gladiators with him, but later over 40,000 runaway slaves joined his forces.

18 Spartacus was a gladiator from the kingdom of Thrace. He joined the Roman army, but did not like it and tried to run away. As a punishment, Spartacus was sent to train as a gladiator, although he was allowed to take his wife with him.

19 The gladiators, led by Spartacus, defeated the Roman army. After breaking out of the gladiator school (called a ludus), Spartacus hid on the slopes of Mount Vesuvius, near Naples. He defeated a small Roman force sent to capture him and then led his growing army to northern Italy. There, at Modena, he defeated a large Roman army and stole valuable goods.

20 Spartacus wanted to cross the Alps, a large mountain range. After winning the battle at Modena, Spartacus wanted to return to Thrace. However, his men wanted to raid cities. They made Spartacus lead them back to southern Italy.

21 The wrong general was credited for defeating Spartacus. Spartacus and his army of slaves and gladiators were defeated by a new Roman army at Lucania. This army was commanded by Marcus Licinius Crassus. One small group of slaves fled the battle and was captured by a commander named Gnaeus Pompey. He then rode to Rome and announced that he had defeated the rebels.

◀ The 1960 movie *Spartacus* starred Kirk Douglas (centre) as the escaped gladiator. Spartacus equipped his army of gladiators and slaves with weapons stolen from the Romans.

Caesar's games

22 **Julius Caesar borrowed money to buy his gladiators.** Caesar rose to become the ruler of the Roman Empire. Early in his career he staged spectacular games to win votes in elections. But Caesar was too poor to afford to pay the bills, so he borrowed money from richer men. When he won the elections, Caesar repaid the men with favours and titles.

▲ Julius Caesar (102–44 BC) was a politician who won several elections after staging magnificent games to entertain the voters.

23 **Caesar's gladiators fought in silver armour.** In 65 BC, Julius Caesar staged the funeral games for his father, who had died 20 years earlier. Caesar was standing for election to be chief priest of Rome. To make his games even more special, Caesar dressed his 640 gladiators in armour made of solid silver.

24 **Caesar brought war elephants to Rome.** In 46 BC Julius Caesar celebrated a victory in North Africa by staging gladiatorial games in Rome. Among the prisoners of war forced to fight in the arena were 40 war elephants, together with the men trained to fight them.

▲ War elephants were popular attractions, and gladiators were specially trained in how to fight against them.

25 Caesar turned senators (governors of Rome) into gladiators. On one occasion Caesar forced two rich noblemen to fight in the arena. They had been sentenced to death by a court, but Caesar ordered that the man who killed the other in the arena could go free.

26 Caesar's final show was too big for the arena. The games staged by Julius Caesar when he wanted to become dictator of Rome were the grandest ever held. After weeks of shows and feasts, the final day saw a fight between two armies of 500 infantry (foot soldiers) and 30 cavalry. The battle was so large it had to be held in the enormous chariot race course, Circus Maximus.

QUIZ

1. Did Caesar's gladiators wear armour made of silver, gold or bronze?
2. Was Caesar's final show a big or small show?
3. Where did Caesar get the money to buy gladiators?

Answers:
1. Silver 2. It was a big show 3. He borrowed money from richer men

▲ Chariot racing was a hugely popular sport that thrilled the crowds in ancient Rome.

The mob

27 **The Roman mob could overpower emperors.** Over a million people lived in ancient Rome. Many were voting citizens who did not have regular jobs. Even the most powerful emperors had to keep this vast mob of Romans happy. If an emperor did not put on impressive gladiatorial shows he could be booed, attacked or even killed.

▲ Emperor Vitellius (AD 69) was murdered by a mob of Romans after failing to put on any impressive games.

◄ The seats in the arena were numbered and cushions were sometimes provided for extra comfort.

28 Each seat was saved for a particular person. People attending the gladiator games had their own seats. The row and seat number were written on small clay tablets that were handed out by the organizer of the games. Some seats were given to whoever queued up outside the arena.

29 Women in ancient Rome could not vote, so they were given seats at the back of the crowd. The best seats were reserved for the men who could vote and had money to help the editor (the man who staged gladiatorial games).

◄ A wounded gladiator pleads for his life by raising the first finger of his left hand. The thumbs-down signal from the mob indicates that he should die.

30 The mob decided which gladiators lived, and which died. A wounded gladiator could appeal for mercy by holding up the first finger of his left hand. The mob gave a thumbs-down gesture if they thought the gladiator should die, or hid their thumbs in clenched fists if they thought he should live. The editor usually did what the mob wanted because he wanted them to vote for him.

I DON'T BELIEVE IT!

Poor Roman citizens were given free bread by the government. In one month in 44 BC, more than 330,000 men queued up to receive this free handout of food.

Amazing arenas

31 The first gladiator fights took place in the cattle market. The cattle market, or Forum Boarium, was a large open space by the river Tiber. Cattle pens were cleared away to make space for fighting, while the audience watched from shops and temples.

◄ The crowd watched early gladiatorial fights in the cattle market from shops and pavements.

32 Most fights took place in the Forum. This was the largest open square in the centre of Rome. The most important temples and government buildings stood around the Forum. After about 150 BC, gladiatorial games were held in the Forum and temporary wooden stands were erected in which spectators could sit.

33 One fight took place in a swivelling arena. In 53 BC, the politician Gaius Scribonius Curio put on a gladiator show and impressed the crowd by staging two plays in back-to-back theatres. The theatres swivelled around to form an arena for a small gladiator show. The crowd loved the new idea and Curio went on to win several elections.

34

The first purpose-built arena had the emperor's name carved on it. In 29 BC an amphitheatre (an open-air building with rows of seats, one above the other) was built to the north of Rome by the politician Titus Statilius Taurus. The amphitheatre was built of stone and timber to replace temporary wooden stands in the Forum. Taurus wanted to impress Emperor Augustus so he carved the name 'Augustus' over the entrance.

▼ The name Augustus dominated the entrance to the arena built by Taurus.

TRUE OR FALSE?

1. The cattle market was the largest open space in Rome.
2. At first spectators watched from shops and temples.
3. Some arenas were round, some oval and some square.

Answers:
1. FALSE The Forum was the largest open space in Rome 2. TRUE Early gladiatorial fights took place in the cattle market and spectators watched from nearby buildings 3. FALSE All arenas were oval

▼ All gladiatorial stadiums were oval in shape, with blocks of seating rising from the central arena.

Seating for less important citizens

Seating for senators and important people

Seating for the editor

Gladiators' exit

Arena

Gladiators' entrance

Seating for women and slaves

35

Every arena had the same layout. Arenas were oval with an entrance at each end. The gladiators came into the arena through one entrance, and the other was reserved for servants and for carrying out any dead gladiators. The editor sat in a special section of the seating called the tribunal editoris, which was on the north side in the shade.

The mighty Colosseum

36 The Colosseum was named after a statue. The official name of the Colosseum was the Flavian Amphitheatre, named after the dynasty of emperors who ordered it to be built. Most ordinary Romans called it the Colosseum because it was built next to the Colossus, a 30-metre-tall statue of Emperor Nero.

Wooden masts

Awning

▶ The Colosseum had complex underground passageways in which gladiators and wild animals were kept before they appeared in the games.

37 The Colosseum was built on a marsh. When Emperor Vespasian Flavian ordered building work to begin in AD 72, there was only one piece of land large enough in Rome that had not already been built on. This was an area of marsh between the river Tiber and the emperor's palace. Before building work could begin the marsh had to be drained.

Stairs leading to seating areas

Underground entrance to arena

38 **The Colosseum could seat 50,000 spectators.** The huge seating area was divided into over 80 sections. Each section had a door and flight of steps that led to the outside of the Colosseum. The standing room at the top was reserved for slaves and may have held another 4000 people.

39 **The Colosseum was probably the largest building in the world.** The outer walls stood 46 metres tall and covered an area 194 metres long by 160 metres wide. The walls were covered in stone, but the structure was made of brick or concrete.

40 **The first games in the Colosseum lasted 100 days.** The Colosseum was finished in AD 80, during the reign of Emperor Titus. He wanted to show that he was the most generous man ever to live in Rome, so he organized gladiatorial games to last for 100 days. Thousands of gladiators and animals fought in these games.

Tiered seating

Trapdoors

Arena floor

Network of corridors and machinery beneath arena floor

Who were the gladiators?

41 **Gladiators were divided into types based on their weapons.** Not all gladiators used the same weapons or fought in the same way. Some gladiators fought with weapons that had been popular in other countries or were used by different types of soldiers. Others used weapons and armour that were made especially for the arena.

Murmillo

42 **Murmillo gladiators used army weapons and military armour.** Their shields and swords were similar to those used by infantry in the Roman army. The shield was one metre long and 65 centimetres wide. The sword was used for stabbing, not cutting.

43 **Thracian gladiators used lightweight armour.** The weapons of the Thracians were based on those used by soldiers from the kingdom of Thrace. The shield was small and square and the leg armour had long metal guards. The sword had a curved blade and the helmets were decorated with a griffin's head (a griffin was an imaginary bird).

Thracian

◄ ▲ ► Thracian, Murmillo and Provocator gladiators were all equipped with armour and heavy weapons. They usually fought each other, sometimes in teams. The lightly equipped Retiarius only had a net and trident.

44 Provocator gladiators wore the heaviest armour of all gladiators. They had a breastplate that protected the chest, a round helmet and leg armour that reached above the knees. The shield was about 80 centimetres long and 60 centimetres wide. They used a short, stabbing sword with a straight blade.

Retiarius

Provocator

MAKE A SHIELD

You will need:
cardboard   scissors
string   coloured paints

1. Take the sheet of cardboard and cut out a rectangular shape with rounded corners.
2. Ask an adult to make a pair of holes close to each long side and tie string through them to make handles.
3. Paint the front of the shield with a bright, colourful design.

45 Retiarius gladiators had a fishing net and trident. These gladiators wore very little armour. They relied on speed and skill to escape attacks from heavily equipped gladiators, such as the provocator gladiators. The fishing net was used to try to trip or entangle an opponent. The trident, a spear with three points, was usually used by fishermen.

Special fighters

◀ The equite gladiators began their combat on horseback, but if one fell off his horse, the other had to fight on foot as well.

46 Equite gladiators were equipped in the same way as the Roman army's cavalry. They used a small, leather shield, a medium-length sword and a lance about 2.5 metres long. Only the helmet was different from that of the army. The army helmet had an open face and no brim. Whenever these gladiators appeared in a show, they were the first to fight.

47 Female gladiators were rare. They first appeared around AD 55 in Rome as a novelty act. They fought only against other women or animals. Female gladiators were banned in AD 200.

▲ Female gladiators fought in the same style as the male gladiators.

48 The andabatae (an-dab-AH-tie) fought blindfolded. The Romans loved anything new or unusual. Andabatae gladiators wore helmets with no eye-holes. They listened carefully for sounds of their opponent, then attacked with two swords. Sometimes the andabatae would fight on horseback.

49 British gladiators fought from chariots. Known as the essedarii (ess-e-DAH-ree-ee), meaning chariot-man, these gladiators first appeared after Julius Caesar invaded Britain in 55 BC. The first chariot gladiators were prisoners of war.

▲ Andabatae helmets had no eye-holes – the gladiators had to rely on their hearing.

ANDABATAE FIGHT

Recreate the combat of the andabatae with this game.

You will need:
blindfold   four or more players

1. One player is the andabatae. Tie on the blindfold, making sure the player can see nothing.
2. Other players run around the andabatae calling out their name.
3. The andabatae tries to catch someone. When they catch a person, that person puts on the blindfold and becomes the andabatae. The game continues for as long as you like.

50 Special clowns who fought with wooden weapons were known as paegniarii (payeg-nee-AH-ree-ee). They appeared at shows during gaps between gladiator fights. They were skilled acrobats and would sometimes tell jokes or make fun of important people in the audience.

▶ The paegniarii used wooden weapons and put on comic displays to entertain the crowd between gladiator fights.

Recruiting gladiators

51 **The first gladiators were household slaves.** The will of the dead man who was being honoured by the games would name his slaves who were to fight. They were made to fight during the funeral. Those who were killed were then buried with their owner.

AUGUSTUS
JULIUS
SPARTACUS
CLAUDIUS

▲ Before a show, the names of the gladiators who were to fight were written on a scroll.

SPQR

CASSIUS SCRIBONIUS

CRIME
ROBBERY

SENTENCE
THREE YEARS
AS GLADIATOR

◄ When convicted, the name, crime and sentence of each criminal was inscribed on a tablet.

I DON'T BELIEVE IT!

When the lanista wanted to buy slaves to become gladiators, he would choose big, strong men. On average a gladiator was about 5 centimetres taller than an ordinary Roman.

52 Criminals could be sent to the arena. The Romans did not have prisons so criminals were usually fined, flogged or executed. Men guilty of some crimes might be ordered to become gladiators for a set period of time – such as three years for robbery. These men would be given a tablet showing the details of their crime and sentence.

53 Some gladiators were volunteers.

These volunteers were often former soldiers who wanted to earn money for their retirement. They signed up for a period of time or for a set number of fights and received a large payment of money if they survived.

54 Gladiators were recruited by the lanista.

Every gladiator school was run by the lanista, the owner and chief trainer. The lanista decided who to recruit and how to train them. He would choose the strongest men to fight in heavy armour and the quickest men to fight as Retiarius gladiators.

◄ Slaves for sale were paraded in front of potential buyers. They were sold to the highest bidder.

55 Strong slaves were sold to become gladiators.

In ancient Rome, slaves were treated as property, and had no human rights. If a man wanted to raise money, he might sell a slave. The lanista would pay a high price for strong male slaves. Many young slaves were also sold to become gladiators.

► The price of slaves varied, but a slave might cost about the same as an average workman's wages for a year.

Learning to fight

56 Gladiators lived in a special training school called a ludus. Most early schools were located near Naples, but they later moved to Rome. Some schools specialized in a particular type of gladiator, but others trained all types. The school was run by the lanista, and some were owned by wealthy noblemen.

▲ Wooden training swords were the same size as real weapons.

57 Gladiators trained with wooden weapons. The weapons made sure that gladiators were not seriously injured during training. It also made it more difficult for gladiators to organize a rebellion, as Spartacus had done. Some wooden weapons were bound with heavy lead weights so that when gladiators fought with normal weapons they could fight for longer.

◀ Most arenas and gladiator schools had a small shrine dedicated to the war god Mars.

58 A special oath (promise) was taken by trainee gladiators in front of a shrine to the gods. The oath made the gladiator obey the lanista without question or endure branding, flogging, chains or death. Gladiators were allowed to keep any prize money they won.

59 New trainees fought against a wooden post called a palus. A trainer, known as a doctor, taught the recruits how to use their weapons and shields to strike at the 2-metre-high wooden post. Only when the basic tactics had been learned did the recruits practise against other gladiators.

▼ Gladiators trained for several hours every day, being instructed on fighting techniques by retired gladiators and more experienced men.

60 The buildings of a gladiator school were constructed around a square training ground. This was where the gladiators did most of their training, exercises and other activities. Around the training ground were rooms where the gladiators lived. Recruits slept in dormitories, but fully trained gladiators had their own rooms.

Armour, shields and helmets

61 Gladiator helmets were decorated with colourful plumes and crests. These were made from coloured feathers or dyed horsehair and made the gladiators look taller and bigger. Sometimes gladiators fought in teams and wore colours to show which team they belonged to.

Secutor

Thracian

▲ Gladiator helmets were highly polished and often decorated with plumes or crests to make them look more impressive.

62 Gladiator armour was heavier than military armour. The shields, helmets and other armour were designed to protect them from their opponent's weapons. Because gladiators wore their armour for a fight that lasted only a few minutes, the armour was thick and heavy to provide extra protection. As soldiers might have to march for hours, they wore lighter armour.

Murmillo

63 **Some armour was covered with gold.** Most gladiator armour was decorated with carvings and reliefs of gods such as Mars, god of war, or Victory, goddess of success. These decorations were often coated with thin sheets of pure gold.

64 **Padded armour was worn on the arms and legs.** Thick layers of cloth and padding gave protection from glancing blows from the weapons or from being hit by the shield of the opponent.

Leather binding

Final shape

Cloth padding

▲ Gladiator shields were painted and decorated with gold to impress the audience.

▲ Arms and legs were often covered with layers of woollen cloth tied on with leather bindings.

I DON'T BELIEVE IT!

Gladiator helmets were very heavy — they weighed about 7 kilograms, twice as much as an army helmet!

65 **The body was usually left without any armour at all.** This meant that a single blow could kill them, or injure them so seriously that they had to ask for mercy. Gladiators needed to be skilful with both weapons and shields to survive.

A day in the life...

66 Gladiators were woken at dawn to begin training. They had several servants to look after them, usually boys or old men. A servant would wake the gladiator at sunrise to make sure he was ready to begin his training on time.

▲ A gladiator would be awoken at dawn by one of the slaves owned by the training school.

67 Training lasted for hours each day. Even the most experienced gladiator began his day practising weapon strokes at a wooden post. This allowed the fighter to warm up, ready for the more serious training later in the day. Gladiators had special plain armour and blunt weapons to use when training.

▼ A stout wooden post about 2 metres tall was used for the more basic training exercises.

GLADIATOR MEAL

Ask an adult to help you prepare this gladiator meal.

You will need:
60 g rolled porridge oats
400 ml water   pinch of salt
50 g ham   5 dried figs
2 tbsp olive oil
1 tsp dried rosemary

1. Chop the ham and figs. Fry in the olive oil and rosemary.
2. Place the oats, water and salt in a saucepan. Bring to the boil, then simmer for 5 minutes.
3. When the oats have thickened, scatter over the ham and figs.

◄ Gladiators were given simple, nutritious food such as porridge, carrots and sausages to keep them fit and healthy.

68 **Barley porridge was the usual food of gladiators, but they also ate meats, fruits and vegetables.** The Romans believed that barley was a highly nutritious food that helped to build up muscles. The owner of the gladiator school did not waste money on fancy foods, but provided plain and healthy meals.

▼ Gladiators were sometimes given treatment by masseurs, doctors and other specialists who looked after their health.

69 **Gladiators received regular massages.** Romans knew that massages would help to ease stiff joints or relax muscles. Massages could be very helpful to old injuries. The gladiator school would employ at least one man who was an expert masseur to keep the gladiators in top condition.

70 **Older, retired gladiators trained the new recruits.** Gladiators who survived long enough to win their freedom often found jobs at gladiator schools. They were expert fighters and knew many tricks and special moves. They trained the new recruits to be expert fighters. This would please the crowd, and give the gladiator a better chance of surviving.

Get ready for the games

71 The first decision when staging gladiatorial games (munus) was how much money to spend. The man who hosted the event was known as the editor. A munus was an expensive event but most editors wanted to put on the most impressive show possible. They would spend as much money as they could spare.

72 The editor would choose different features for his show. A lanista would be hired to organize the show. Together, they would decide how many gladiators would fight and how many musicians and other performers were needed. The lanista would make sure the event was a success.

▲ Musicians and dancers were popular at gladiator shows. Shows often included a parade of entertainers before the gladiators.

73 A dead gladiator cost more than a wounded one. The editor would sign a contract with the lanista. This set down everything that would appear at the munus and the cost. If a gladiator was killed, a special payment was made so that the lanista could buy and train a replacement. Many editors granted mercy to a wounded man to avoid paying extra.

74 Everything was hired – even the clothes worn by the organizer. The editor would hire expensive clothes and jewellery for himself and his family. He wanted to make sure that they looked their best when they appeared at the games. The editor wanted to impress his fellow citizens and make sure they would vote for him.

▼ Smart clothes were hired for the editor and his family so that they could show off to the audience.

75 The star of the show was the editor. Everything was arranged so that the editor of the games looked as important as possible. As well as wearing special clothes, he was given the most prominent seat in the amphitheatre and all the gladiators and other performers bowed to him. He was paying for the show and wanted to make sure he got all the credit.

A laurel wreath signified an honour granted by the Roman government

A toga was a special item of clothing that indicated the wearer's rank within society

Gold jewellery indicated a family's wealth

Brightly coloured silk from China showed wealth and sophistication

Purple was the most expensive dye in ancient Rome

Showtime!

76 **Advertising for the show began days beforehand.** The lanista sent out slaves to paint signs on walls, while others shouted announcements on the street. The slaves told people when and where the show was and what it included. They also told them the name of the editor of the show.

77 **The show began with a parade, which was led into the arena by the editor.** He was dressed in beautiful clothes and often rode in a chariot. Behind him came the musicians playing lively tunes. Then came the gladiators, each followed by a slave who carried the gladiator's weapons and armour. Then came statues of gods including the war god Mars. Finally the servants, referees and other officials entered the arena.

78 **Gladiators were carefully paired against each other.** Before the show began, the editor and lanista would decide which gladiators would fight each other. The show would start with beginners fighting each other, with the expert veterans appearing towards the end of the show. The results would be shouted out by a herald and written on a sign, or tabella, at one end of the arena.

79 **The probatio was a crucial ceremony.** Before the first fight of the show, the editor and lanista would enter the arena for the probatio. This ceremony involved the men testing the weapons and armour to be used in the show. Swords were tested by slicing up vegetables, and armour by being hit with clubs.

◄ Each gladiator show began with a grand parade of everyone involved in the show, led by the editor in a chariot.

80 **Musicians performed first.** The band included trumpets, curved horns and the hydraulis. This was a loud instrument like a modern church organ. The musicians entertained the crowd between fights and played music during the show ceremonies.

TRUE OR FALSE?

1. The hydraulis was an instrument like a modern trumpet.

2. Weapons were tested before the show to make sure they were sharp.

3. Gladiators wore their armour during the opening parade.

Answers:
1. FALSE The hydraulis was an instrument like a modern organ 2. TRUE Weapons were tested during the probatio ceremony 3. FALSE Slaves carried the armour behind the gladiators

Water fights

81 Some gladiatorial shows took place on water. The most impressive of all were the naumachiae, or sea fights. For these shows, an artificial lake 557 metres long by 536 metres wide was dug beside the river Tiber. Small warships were brought up the river and launched on the lake when a sea fight was due to take place.

82 Naval fights were recreations of real battles. In 2 BC, Emperor Augustus staged a naumachia that recreated a battle fought 400 years earlier between the Greeks and the Persians. Emperor Titus staged a battle that originally started between the Greeks and Egyptians. These battles did not always end with the same winner as the real battle.

▼ Recreated naval battles were extremely expensive to stage, so didn't take place very often.

83 **The first naval gladiators did not try to kill each other.** The first of the sea battles were staged by Julius Caesar to celebrate a naval victory. The show was designed to impress the audience with the skills of the sailors and the way Caesar had won his victory.

84 **One naval show involved 19,000 men.** Emperor Claudius staged a sea battle on Lake Fucino. The men fighting were not sailors or gladiators but criminals condemned to death. Most of the men died and any survivors were sent to work as slaves.

85 **The Colosseum in Rome could be flooded for naval fights.** When the Colosseum was first built it had special pipes that could fill the arena with water and then drain it away again. The flooded arena was used for fights between special miniature warships crewed by gladiators. Later, the pipes were replaced by trapdoors and stage scenery.

I DON'T BELIEVE IT!

On one occasion, gladiators took one look at the poor condition of the warships and refused to board them.

Wild animal hunts

86 The first wild animal show was to celebrate a military victory. In 164 BC Rome defeated the powerful North African city of Carthage. The victorious general, Publius Cornelius Scipio, was given the nickname Africanus. He brought back to Rome hundreds of African wild animals, such as elephants, crocodiles and lions. After parading the animals through the streets, he included them in his gladiatorial games.

▲ This ancient mosaic detail shows a gladiator killing a lion. Wild animals were captured and shipped to Rome to fight in the arenas.

87 One elephant hunt went badly wrong. In 79 BC General Gnaeus Pompey staged a wild elephant hunt with 20 elephants in a temporary arena in Rome. The crowd was protected by a tall iron fence, but two of the elephants charged at the fence, smashing it down. The elephants were quickly killed by hunters, but several people were injured.

88 The design of the arena changed to make it safer for the crowds. As the wild animal shows became more popular, the need to keep the watching crowd safe meant changes to the arena had to be made. The arena was sunk about 3 metres into the ground and surrounded by a vertical wall of smooth stone. No animal could leap up the wall or break it down, so the spectators were safe from attack.

89 **Some animal shows were fantastic and strange.** The Romans loved to see animals fighting each other. Sometimes a group of lions or wolves would be set to attack zebras or deer. At other times two hunting animals would be made to fight each other. They were often chained together to encourage them to fight. Some pairings were very odd – a snake was set against a lion, a seal set to fight a wolf or a bull against a bear.

90 **One of the most popular animal fights was when a lion was set against a tiger.** So many lions and tigers were sent to Rome to die in the fights that they became extinct in some areas of North Africa and the Middle East.

I DON'T BELIEVE IT!

The Romans loved watching animals that had been trained to perform tricks. One animal trainer put on shows in which an ape drove a chariot pulled by camels.

▼ A wild tiger attacks a gladiator, as seen in the 2000 movie *Gladiator*. Wild animals were part of most arena shows.

Outside Rome

91 More gladiators fought in southern Italy than in Rome. The idea of gladiatorial fights came from Campania, the area of Italy around Naples. For hundreds of years, the gladiator schools in Campania produced the best-trained gladiators and had more than anywhere else. One school had over 5000 gladiators training at one time.

92 The city of London had a small arena for gladiatorial games and other events. It stood inside the city walls beside the army fortress, near what is now St Paul's Cathedral. The 30-metre-long amphitheatre was built of stone and timber and could seat around 4000 spectators. St Albans, Chester and Caerleon also had amphitheatres.

▼ The arena at Pompeii. The oval shape, banked seating and two exits were the common design for all arenas.

93 **All gladiatorial shows had to honour the emperor.** By about AD 50, political power was in the hands of the emperor. It was the emperor who decided who could stand for election, and who would win the election. The editor of a gladiator show always began by dedicating the show to the emperor.

94 **The best gladiators were sent to Rome.** Gladiators who fought in provinces such as Britain or Spain were owned by lanistas who travelled from city to city to put on a show. Agents from Rome would watch these shows and any gladiator who was particularly good would be taken to Rome to fight in the Colosseum.

◀ A statue of an emperor. Such a statue stood in most arenas and other public buildings.

▼ A gladiator fight reaches its end, as seen in the 1960 movie *Spartacus*.

95 **Some towns banned gladiators.** Not everyone enjoyed the fights. Many Romans refused to attend the games. Some cities, particularly in Greece and the eastern provinces, did not have an amphitheatre and refused to put on combats. Some people thought the fights were a waste of good slaves.

The last gladiators

▲ A scene from the 2000 movie *Gladiator*. The bloodshed in gladiator fights appalled some Romans.

96 Gladiatorial games became less and less popular. Seneca, a wise man and a great thinker, wrote that attending the games made Romans more cruel and inhuman than they had been before. The writer Artemidorus of Daldis said that the games were dishonourable, cruel and wicked. However, most Romans approved of the games and enjoyed watching them.

97 In AD 324, Christian bishops tried to ban gladiatorial fights. After AD 250, Christianity became popular in the Roman Empire. Christians believed that the fights were sinful and they asked Emperor Constantine I to ban the fights. He banned private games, but allowed state games to continue.

98 In AD 366 Pope Damasus used gladiators to murder rival churchmen. When Pope Liberius died the cardinals of Rome could not agree on a successor. Followers who wanted Ursinus to be the next pope were meeting in the church of St Maria Trastevere when Damasus hired a gang of gladiators to attack them. The gladiators broke into the church and killed 137 people. Damasus then became pope.

99 The Christian monk Telemachus was the first to stop a gladiator fight. During a show in the Colosseum in AD 404, Telemachus forced apart two fighting gladiators. He made a speech asking for the shows to stop, but angry spectators killed him. Emperor Honorius then closed down all the gladiator schools in Rome.

▲ Heavily armed gladiators were sometimes hired by ambitious politicians and churchmen to murder their rivals.

100 The last gladiators fought in around AD 445. In AD 410, the city of Rome was captured by a tribe of barbarians. The Roman Empire was falling to pieces. People were too busy trying to escape invasions or to earn a living to organize gladiatorial fights.

◀ The monk Telemachus managed to stop a gladiator fight, but paid for his actions with his life.

VIKINGS

Map labels:
- GREENLAND
- ICELAND
- CANADA
- NEWFOUNDLAND
- Compass: N, S, E, W

101 **The Vikings lived in Scandinavia over 1000 years ago.** They spread terror throughout Europe from around AD 800 to 1100. Viking warriors made fierce raids on peaceful villages, battled to win new land, and plundered treasures and snatched people to sell as slaves. Viking merchants travelled vast distances through Europe to the Middle East, selling jewellery and fine goods. Viking families set up farms in England, Ireland, Scotland and France while explorers sailed west to start new settlements in Iceland, Greenland and Russia – and were the first Europeans to reach North America, around AD 1000.

▼ This map shows Viking homelands, settlements and routes of travel. The Vikings' name meant 'pirates', 'port-attackers', or 'people of the bays' – historians do not know for sure. Whichever meaning is true, it tells us that Vikings spent their lives close to the sea. They were some of the world's best, bravest sailors.

KEY

Viking homelands

Viking settlements

Viking routes

NORWAY

SWEDEN

IRELAND

RUSSIA

BRITAIN

DENMARK

GERMANY

FRANCE

ITALY

SPAIN

BYZANTINE EMPIRE

Kings and people

102 Viking society had three classes. At the top were nobles (kings or chiefs). They were rich, owned land and had many servants. Freemen, the middle group, included farmers, traders, and craftworkers and their wives. Slaves were the lowest group. They worked hard for nobles and freemen and could not leave their owner.

Viking slave

Viking farmer

Viking noble warrior

▲ Slaves, farmers and warriors all worked hard to make Viking lands rich and powerful.

◄ Famous for his cruelty, Erik Bloodaxe was the last Viking to rule the kingdom of Northumbria, in north-east England.

103 Viking warlords turned into kings. During early Viking times, local chiefs controlled large areas of land. They also had armies of freemen. Over the centuries, some nobles became richer and more powerful than the rest by raiding and conquering foreign lands. By AD 1050, just one noble controlled each Viking country, and called himself king.

104 King Erik Bloodaxe killed his brothers. When a Viking king died, each of his sons had an equal right to inherit the throne. Members of Viking royal families often had to fight among themselves for the right to rule. In AD 930, King Erik of Norway killed his brothers so that he could rule alone.

105

King Harald Bluetooth left a magnificent memorial.
King Harald ruled Denmark from around AD 935 to 985. He was one of the first Viking kings to become a Christian. He built a church at Jelling, the ancient Danish royal burial site, and had his parents' bodies dug up and re-buried inside. He also paid for a splendid pyramid-shaped monument to be built next to the church, in memory of them. This 'Jelling Stone' was decorated with carvings in Viking and Christian designs.

▶ The Jelling stone (far right) has carvings of a snake and a lion–like monster, fighting each other. They symbolize the forces of good and evil.

106

King Cnut ruled a European empire – but not the waves. King Cnut was one of the mightiest Viking kings. By 1028 he ruled England, Denmark and Norway. However he did not want to appear too proud. So, one day, he staged a strange event on an English beach and commanded the waves to obey him. When they did not he said, 'This proves that I am weak. Only God can control the sea.'

I DON'T BELIEVE IT!
Many Viking rulers had strange or violent names, such as Svein Forkbeard, Einar Falsemouth, Magnus Barelegs, Thorfinn Skullsplitter and Sigurd the Stout.

51

Sailors and raiders

107 Vikings sailed in dragon ships. There were different kinds of ships. Cargo ships were slow and heavy, with wide, deep hulls to carry loads. Ferry and river boats were small and sturdy, with lots of room for passengers. The most splendid ships were *drakkar* (dragon ships), designed for war. They were long, slender and fast, with a beautifully carved stern and prow. Their shallow keels helped them land quickly on beaches to make raids.

Steering oar at stern

Rowers sat on benches, one man to each oar

QUIZ

1. What were *drakkar*?
2. When did Svein Forkbeard rule Denmark?
3. What kind of wood was used to make the keel of a boat?

Answers:
1. Viking ships
2. AD 985–1014 3. Oak

108 Sailors steered by the stars. The Vikings had no radio or satellite systems to help them navigate (steer a course) when they were out of sight of land. So they made careful observations of the Sun by day and the stars by night, to work out their position. They also studied the winds, waves and ocean currents, and the movements of fish and seabirds.

Square sail made of linen or wool

109 Shipbuilders searched for tall

trees. They used oak timbers to make the keel (backbone) of each vessel. The biggest keels came from trees at least 40 metres high. Shipbuilders added long overlapping planks of oak, ash or birch, to make the hull. For masts, they used the trunks of very tall, straight trees, such as pine.

Carved wooden prow

▼ A Viking dragon ship. Its long, sleek hull is made of overlapping planks of wood, held together with iron nails. Its tall mast is made from a single pine tree.

110 Pirates demanded

gold to go away. Viking pirates such as King Svein Forkbeard of Denmark (ruled AD 985–1014) demanded money with menaces. He led Viking warships to England and promised to attack if he was not paid to sail away. Svein's tactics worked. Each time he returned, the English handed over 'Dane-geld' (gold for the Danes) – again and again.

Strong wooden keel (helped steer a swift, straight course through the waves)

111 Raiders carried off treasure and

slaves. Viking nobles recruited gangs of loyal warriors to go on raiding expeditions. They sailed away from Viking homelands to attack villages or defenceless monasteries. Their aim was to grab valuable treasure and healthy young men and women to sell as slaves.

▼ Families living in seaside villages lived in constant fear of a Viking pirate raid.

Warriors and weapons

112 Vikings valued glory more than long life. They believed that a dead warrior's fame lived on after him, and made sure that his name would never die. Myths and legends also told how warriors who died in battle would go to Valhalla, where they feasted with the gods.

113 Berserkirs were mad for battle. Berserkirs ('bear-shirts') were warriors who dressed in animal skins and worked themselves into a trance before battle. They charged at the enemy, howling and growling like wolves and biting at their shields. In this state, they were wild and fearless and dangerous to anyone who got in their way. This is where the word 'beserk' comes from.

▲ Berserkir warriors rushed madly into battle, wearing animal skins over their chain mail armour.

114 Lords led followers into war. There were no national armies in Viking times. Each king or lord led his followers into battle against a shared enemy. A lord's followers fought to win praise, plus rich rewards, such as arm rings of silver or a share of captured loot.

115 Warriors gave names to their swords. A good sword was a Viking warrior's most treasured possession. He gave it a name such as 'Sharp Biter', and often asked to be buried with it. Viking swords were double-edged, with strong, flexible blades made by hammering layers of iron together. Their hilts (handles) were decorated with patterns in silver and gold.

116 Viking soldiers lived in camps and forts. Wars and raids took warriors far from home. Soldiers in places such as England built camps of wooden huts, surrounded by an earth bank topped by a wooden wall.

A round shield, made of wood covered with leather; a metal 'boss' (centre panel) protected the warrior's hand

Long sword

Knife

Decorated iron helmet, with a protective metal mask around the eyes

Long, sharp spear

I DON'T BELIEVE IT!

Viking women went to war but they did not fight. Instead, they nursed wounded warriors and cooked meals for hungry soldiers.

▲ Each Viking soldier had to provide his own weapons and armour. Poor soldiers wore leather caps and tunics, and carried knives and spears. Wealthy Vikings could afford metal helmets and tunics, and fine, sharp swords.

The Vikings at home

117 In the 700s and 800s, the Vikings were some of the best craftworkers in Europe. They lived in a harsh environment, with cold, long, dark winters. Buildings were needed to shelter livestock, as well as people. In towns, pigs, goats and horses were kept in sheds, but in parts of the countryside, farmers built longhouses, with rooms for the family at one end and space for animals at the other.

118 Vikings built houses out of grass. In many lands where the Vikings settled, such as the Orkney Islands or Iceland, there were hardly any trees. So Viking families built homes out of slabs of turf (earth with grass growing in it), arranged on a low foundation of stone. If they could afford it, they lined the rooms with planks of wood imported from Scandinavia. Otherwise, they collected pieces of driftwood washed up on shore.

Animals were kept in the longhouse

Loom for weaving cloth

Walls made of logs

▶ Longhouses were usually built on sloping ground so that waste from the animals ran downhill, away from human living quarters.

119 Viking homes could be unhealthy.

Their houses did not have windows – they would have let in too much cold. So homes were often damp, and full of smoke from the fire burning on the hearth. As a result, Viking people suffered from chest diseases. Some may also have been killed by a poisonous gas called carbon monoxide, which is produced when a fire uses up all the oxygen in a room.

I DON'T BELIEVE IT!

Vikings liked living in longhouses, because heat from the animals provided a kind of central heating, keeping everyone warm.

Turf (earth with growing grass) roof

Wooden rafters

Meat was smoked to preserve it

120 Homeowners sat in the high seat.

Most Viking families had little furniture. Only the rich could afford beds, or tables with fixed legs. Most homes were simply furnished with trestle tables, wooden storage chests and wooden benches. The centre of one bench was marked off by two carved wooden pillars, and reserved as the 'high seat' (place of honour) for the house owner. Important guests sat facing him or her, on the bench opposite.

Outside lavatory

Food and famine

121 **Vikings ate two meals a day.** First thing in the morning was the 'day meal' of barley bread or oatcakes, and butter or cheese. The main meal – 'night meal' – was eaten in the early evening. It included meat or fish, plus wild berries in summer. Meals were served on wooden plates or soapstone bowls and eaten with metal knives and wood or horn spoons.

Patterned silver cup
used by the rich

▶ Objects made from cattle horn were light but very strong – ideal for Viking traders or raiders to carry on their journeys.

Pottery beaker
used by the poor

Drinking horn
used by warriors

QUIZ

1. What did Viking warriors drink from?
2. How did the Vikings boil water?
3. What is offal?
4. How long would a feast last for?

Answers:
1. From cattle horns
2. On red-hot stones 3. The heart, liver and lungs of animals 4. A week or more

122 **Warriors drunk from hollow horns.** Favourite Viking drinks were milk, whey (the liquid left over from cheese-making), ale (brewed from malted barley), and mead (honey wine). Rich people drank from glass or silver cups, but ordinary people had wooden or pottery beakers. On special occasions feasts were held, and Viking warriors drank from curved cattle horns.

123 Red-hot stones boiled water for cooking.
Few Viking homes had ovens. So women and their servants boiled meat in iron cauldrons, or in water-filled pits heated by stones that were made red-hot in a fire. This was a very efficient way of cooking.

Cabbage
Beans
Garlic
Peas
Onion

▲ Vegetables eaten by Vikings included peas, beans, cabbages, onions and garlic.

124 The Vikings loved blood sausages.
Cooks made sausages by pouring fresh animal blood and offal (heart, liver and lungs) into cleaned sheep's intestines, then boiling them. Sometimes they added garlic, cumin seeds or juniper berries as flavouring. Vikings preferred these to vegetables such as cabbages, peas and beans.

▼ Viking women and slaves cooked huge meals over open fires, and served them to feasting warriors.

125 Feasts went on for a week or more.
After winning a great victory, Vikings liked to celebrate. Kings and lords held feasts to reward their warriors, and families feasted at weddings. Guests dressed in their best clothes and hosts provided plenty of food and drink. Everyone stayed in the feast hall until the food ran out, or they grew tired.

Skilled craftworkers

126 Vikings made most of the things they needed. Families had to make – and mend – almost everything, from their houses and furniture to farm carts, clothes and children's toys. They had no machines to help them, so most of this work was done slowly and carefully by hand.

127 Blacksmiths travelled from farm to farm. Many Viking men had a simple smithy at home, where they could make and mend tools. For specialized work, they relied on skilled blacksmiths who travelled the countryside, or they made a long journey to a workshop in a town.

▼ Blacksmiths heated iron over open fires until it was soft enough to hammer into shape to make tools and weapons.

128

Bones could be beautiful. Skilled craftworkers used deer antlers to make fine combs. But these were too expensive for ordinary Vikings to buy. They carved bones left over from mealtimes into combs, beads and pins, as well as name tags and weaving tablets (used to make patterned braid).

129

Craftsmen carved cups from the cliff face. Deposits of soft soapstone were found in many Viking lands. It looked good, but it was very heavy. To save taking lumps of it to their workshops, stoneworkers carved rough shapes of cups and bowls into cliffs at soapstone quarries, then took them home to finish neatly.

Handle

Decorated handle

◀ Combs were made by fixing rows of teeth into decorated handles.

Row of bone teeth

130

Silversmiths used special skills. To make a brooch, they hammered a die (a block of metal marked with a brooch design) into a sheet of silver. Then they added detail such as filigree (drops of molten silver) or niello (a black paste pressed into lines scratched on the silver). To make arm- and neck-rings, they twisted silver wires together.

◀ This Viking silver neck-ring is made of thick silver wires, carefully braided together.

Viking towns

131 Kings built towns to encourage trade. Before the Vikings grew so powerful, merchants traded at fairs held just once or twice a year. Viking kings decided to build towns so that trade could continue all year round. Taxes were collected from the people and merchants who traded there.

► Viking markets were often held on beaches. Farming families and travelling merchants met there to buy and sell.

132 Towns were tempting targets for attack. Pirates and raiders from Russia and north Germany sailed across the Baltic Sea to snatch valuable goods from Viking towns. So kings paid for towns to be defended with high banks of earth and strong wooden walls. They also sent troops of warriors to guard them.

133 Houses in towns were specially designed. Space was limited inside town walls so houses were built close together. They were smaller than country homes, as people needed less space to store crops or house animals. Most town houses were made of wood with thatched roofs. Many had craft workshops and showrooms inside.

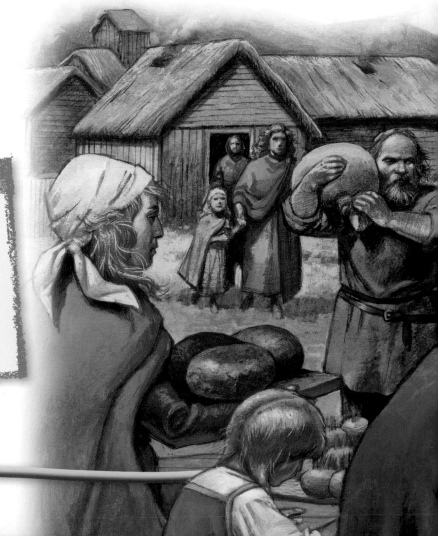

I DON'T BELIEVE IT!

The first Russians were Vikings. The name 'Russia' comes from the word, 'Rus', used by people living east of the Baltic Sea to describe Viking traders who settled there.

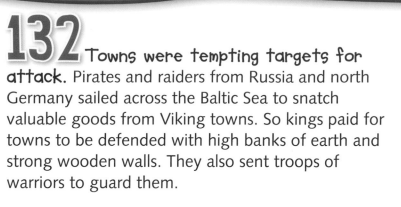

134
Towns made the first Viking coins. As far as we know, there were no coins in Scandinavia before the Viking age. Traders bartered (swapped) goods, or paid for them using bits of silver, weighed out on tiny, portable scales. But many foreign coins came to Viking lands from overseas trading and raiding. Around AD 825, craftsmen in the Viking town of Hedeby (now in north Germany) began to copy them. Later, other towns set up mints to make coins of their own.

135
Viking traders gave Russia its name. Adventurous Vikings visiting the east shores of the Baltic set up towns as bases for trade. Some of the biggest were Staraja Ladoga and Novgorod, in Russia, and Kiev in Ukraine.

◄ This Viking coin shows a merchant ship. It comes from the town of Hedeby.

Law and order

136 Vikings followed a strict code of honour. Men and women were proud and dignified and honour was important to them. It was a disgrace to be called a cheat or a coward, or to run away from a fight. Vikings also prized loyalty. They swore solemn promises to be faithful to lords and comrades and sealed bargains by shaking hands.

137 Many quarrels were settled by fighting. Quarrels between Viking families often led to feuds. If one family member was insulted or killed, all others had a duty to avenge him. Feuds could continue for months, with many people on both sides being killed, until each family was prepared to seek peace and pay compensation.

▲ Viking warriors challenged people who insulted them – or harmed their families – to a deadly duel.

138 Viking laws were not written down.
Instead, they were memorized by a man known as the law-speaker. He recited them out loud every year so that everyone else could hear and understand them. Because of their expert knowledge, law-speakers often became advisors to kings and lords.

139 Every year, Vikings met at the Thing.
This was an open-air assembly of all free men in a district. It met to punish criminals and make new laws. The most usual punishments were heavy fines. Thing meetings were great social occasions where people from remote communities had the chance to meet and exchange news. Many traders also attended, setting up stalls with goods around the edge of a field.

▼ All free men – from noble chieftains to farmers – could speak and vote at a Viking Thing.

140 Ruthlessness was respected.
It was tough being a Viking. Everyone had to work hard to survive and there was no room in the community for people who were weak, lazy or troublesome. Thieves were often hanged and criminals who refused to pay compensation or fines were outlawed. This was a very harsh penalty. Without a home and family, it was hard for any individual to survive.

QUIZ
1. What were the two worst Viking punishments for crimes?
2. How did the Vikings settle family feuds?
3. Why did Vikings shake hands with each other?
4. Who recited the Viking laws?

Answers:
1. Hanging and being outlawed
2. By fighting 3. To seal bargains
4. The law-speaker

Games, music and sport

▲ Vikings loved magical, mysterious tales of dragons, elves and monsters — and exciting stories about famous local heroes.

141 **Vikings liked music, dancing and clowns.** At feasts, Vikings sang songs and danced. Depending on how much the guests had drunk, the dancing might be slow or riotous. Kings and lords also paid dancers, clowns, acrobats and jugglers to entertain their guests at feasts.

142 **Vikings laughed at jokes and riddles.** The Vikings had a rough, quick-witted sense of humour. They liked playing practical jokes and listening to stories about gods and heroes who defeated enemies by trickery. Vikings also played dice and board games such as chess and 'hneftafl' (king's table). But they were not good losers. Fighting often broke out at the end of a game.

▶ This board and counters were probably used for playing the game 'hneftafl', which was rather like chess.

143 Swimming, racing and jumping were favourite summer games. In summer, the weather was warm enough for Vikings to take off most of their clothes. This made it much easier for people to move freely and run and jump at greater speed. In winter, warmly-dressed Vikings liked snow-based sports such as cross-country skiing, as well as ice skating on frozen rivers and lakes.

▼ Viking archers used bows made of yew wood, strung with twisted plant fibres. Arrows were made of birch wood, with sharp tips made of iron.

144 Viking sports were good training for war. Spear-throwing, sword-fighting and archery (shooting at targets with bows and arrows) were all popular Viking sports. They were also excellent training in battle skills and helped boys and young men to develop their body strength, get used to handling weapons and improve their aim.

145 Vikings liked watching wrestling – and fights between horses. Wrestling matches were also good training for war. A warrior who lost his weapons might have to fight for his life on the battlefield. But many Vikings watched wrestling just for fun. They enjoyed the violence. They also liked to watch brutal fights between stallions (male horses), who attacked one another with hooves and teeth.

Gods and goddesses

146 **Viking people honoured many gods.** The Aesir (sky gods) included Odin, Thor and Tyr, who were gods of war, and Loki, who was a trickster. The Vanir (gods of earth and water) included Njord (god of the sea) and Frey (the farmers' god). He and his sister Freyja brought pleasure and fertility.

▼ Odin, Viking god of war, rode an eight-legged horse. Two ravens, called Thought and Memory, flew by his side.

▼ Beautiful Viking goddess Freyja rode in a chariot pulled by cats.

147 **Animals – and people – were killed as sacrifices.** The Vikings believed that they could win favours from the gods by offering them gifts. Since life was the most valuable gift, they gave the gods living sacrifices. Vikings also cooked meals of meat – called blood-offerings – to share with the gods.

148 **Destiny controlled the Vikings.** According to legends, three sisters (Norns) decided what would happen in the world. They sat at the foot of Yggdrasil, the great tree that supported the universe, spinning 'the thread of destiny'. They also visited each newborn baby to decide its future. Once made, this decision could not be changed.

149 After death, Vikings went to Hel's kingdom. Vikings believed that warriors who died in battle went to Valhalla or to Freyja's peaceful home. Unmarried girls also joined Freyja, and good men went to live with gods in the sky. Most Vikings who lived ordinary lives and died of illness or old age could only look forward to a future in Niflheim. This was a gloomy place, shrouded in fog, ruled by a fierce goddess called Hel.

▶ Vikings asked fierce and furious god Tyr to help them win victories.

150 Towards the end of the Viking age, many people became Christians. Missionaries from England, Germany and France visited Viking lands from around AD 725. The Vikings continued to worship their own gods for the next 300 years. Around AD 1000, Viking kings such as Harald Bluetooth and Olaf Tryggvason decided to follow the Christian faith to help strengthen their power. They built churches and encouraged people to become Christians.

▼ Njord was god of the sea. He married the giantess Skadi, who watched over snowy mountains.

QUIZ

1. Who was Loki?
2. What was the name of the tree that was said to support the universe?
3. Where did warriors go when they died?

Answers:
1. A trickster god
2. Yggdrasil 3. Valhalla

Heroes, legends and sagas

151 Vikings honoured heroes who died in battle. They told stories, called 'sagas', about their adventures so that their name and fame never died. These stories were passed on by word of mouth for many years. After the end of the Viking Age, they were written down.

▶ Vikings loved sagas – stories that recorded past events and famous peoples' lives.

152 Skalds sang songs and told saga stories. Viking kings and lords employed their own personal poets, called skalds. A skald's job was to sing songs and recite poems praising his employer, and to entertain guests at feasts. Most skalds played music on harps or lyres to accompany their poems and songs.

▼ Viking legends told how the world would come to an end at the battle of Ragnarok. They also promised that a new world would be born from the ruins of the old.

153 Vikings feared that the world might end. There were many Viking stories foretelling Ragnarok – the Doom of the Gods. This would be a terrible time, when the forces of good clashed with the powers of evil. Viking gods would fight against giants and monsters – and lose. Then the world would come to an end.

154 **The Vikings believed in spirits and monsters.** They were unseen powers that lived in the natural world. Some, such as elves, were kindly and helpful. They sent good harvests and beautiful children. Others, such as giants who ate humans, were wicked or cruel. Vikings often imagined monsters as looking like huge, fierce animals. They carved these monster heads on ships and stones to scare evil spirits away.

▲ Vikings believed that Valkyries — wild warrior women — carried men who had died in battle to live with Odin in Valhalla (the hall of brave dead).

◀ A Viking silver amulet (lucky charm), shaped like Thor's hammer.

QUIZ

1. What did Vikings call the end of the world?
2. Who did skalds praise?
3. Why did farmers wear hammers round their necks?
4. Where did Vikings carve the heads of monsters?

Answers:
1. Ragnarok 2. Their employer 3. To bring fertility to their fields and animals 4. On ships and stones

155 **Lucky charms protected warriors and farmers.** They wore amulets shaped like the god Thor's magic hammer as pendants around their necks. Warriors believed that these amulets would give them strength in battle. Farmers hoped they would bring fertility to their fields and animals.

Death and burial

156 **Early Vikings burned their dead.** At the start of the Viking age, the bodies of dead people were cremated (burned) on big wood fires. After this, their ashes were collected and buried in pottery urns. Between AD 800 and 900, people in some Viking lands began to bury unburned dead bodies in the ground.

157 **Dead men and women took useful items with them to the next world.** The Vikings believed that dead peoples' souls survived to go on living in the next world. So the bodies of dead Viking men and women were surrounded by 'grave goods' – all kinds of things they might need. For rich warriors, this meant clothes, weapons, horses – and sometimes, wives and slaves. Rich women were buried with clothes, jewels, furniture and equipment for spinning and weaving.

158 Viking graves have survived for hundreds of years. Archaeologists have discovered many collections of grave contents, in remarkably good condition. Some, such as jewellery, pottery and stone carvings, are made of materials that do not rot. Some, such as clothing, have survived by chance. Others, such as ship burials, have been preserved underwater. All have provided valuable evidence about life in Viking times.

▼ These stones arranged in the shape of a ship's hull mark an ancient Viking burial ground.

159 Vikings hoped that ships might carry their souls away. So they surrounded buried cremation urns with ship-shaped enclosures of stones. Some enclosures were very large – up to 80 metres long – and were probably also used as places of worship. Very important Viking men and women were cremated or buried in real wooden ships, along with valuable grave goods.

◄ The dead were laid to rest in cloth-covered shelters on board real ships. Then the ships were set on fire so that their souls could 'sail away' to the next world.

160 Vikings treated dead bodies with great respect. They washed them, dressed them and wrapped them in cloth or birch bark before burying them or cremating them. This was because the Vikings believed that dead people might come back to haunt them if they were not treated carefully.

I DON'T BELIEVE IT!

Some Viking skeletons and wooden ships that were buried in acidic soils have been completely eaten away. But they have left 'shadows' in the ground, which archaeologists can use to find out more about them.

The end of the Vikings

161 Kings defeated Viking power. For centuries, kings in England, Scotland and Ireland failed to drive the Vikings from their lands. But after AD 1000, they began to succeed. Brian Boru, high king of Ireland, defeated the Vikings in 1014, and Viking rule ended in England in 1042. Kings of Norway, descended from Vikings, ruled parts of Scotland until 1266 and the Orkney and Shetland Islands until 1469.

▼ On St Brice's Day (13 November, 1002) English King Ethelred II gave orders that Danes living in England should be killed.

162 **Vikings learned to live alongside other peoples.** In most places where Vikings settled, they married local women and worked with local people. Some of their words and customs blended with local ones, but many disappeared. Viking traditions only survived if the place where they settled was uninhabited, such as Iceland, or the Orkney Islands, off the north of Scotland.

▲ In 1066, the Normans – descendants of Vikings who had settled in Normandy, France – invaded and conquered England. This scene from the huge Bayeux Tapestry (embroidered wall-hanging) shows their Viking-style ships.

163 **Christianity destroyed faith in Viking gods.** The Vikings believed their gods, such as Thor and Odin, would punish them if they did not worship them, and would kill Christian missionaries. But the missionaries survived, and so did Vikings who became Christians. This made other Vikings wonder if their gods had any powers, at all.

◀ Christians living in Scandinavia after the end of the Viking age made statues of Jesus Christ to stand in their churches, as symbols of their faith.

164 **Vikings set up new kingdoms outside Viking lands.** In places far away from the Viking homelands, such as Novgorod in Russia, or Normandy in northern France, Viking warlords set up kingdoms that developed independently. Over the years, they lost touch with their Viking origins, and created new customs, laws and lifestyles of their own.

165 **Viking settlers abandoned America.** Soon after AD 1000, Thorfinn Karlsefni, a Viking merchant from Iceland, led over 100 Viking men and women to settle at Vinland – the site in North America where Lief Eriksson landed. They stayed there for two years, but left because the native people attacked them and drove them away.

Viking survivals

166 Some days of the week still have Viking names. The Vikings honoured different gods on different days of the week. We still use some of these gods' names in our calendars. For example, Wednesday means 'Woden's Day', Thursday means 'Thor's Day' and Friday means 'Freyja's Day'. In modern Scandinavian languages, Saturday is called 'bath-day', because that was when the Vikings had their weekly bath!

167 We still use many Viking words today. In countries where the Vikings settled, they spoke Viking languages and gave Viking names to their surroundings. Many Viking words for everyday things still survive such as 'sister', 'knife' and 'egg'. Many places in northern Europe still have Viking names, such as 'Thorpe' (outlying farm), Firth (river estuary), Cape Wrath (Cape Turning-point) or 'Kirkwall' (Church-bay).

168 A Viking story inspired Shakespeare's most famous play. William Shakespeare (1564–1616) lived over 500 years after the Vikings. He used one of their stories to provide the plot for one of his best-known plays. It tells the story of Hamlet, a prince in Denmark, who cannot make up his mind what to do after his father is murdered.

▶ In Shakespeare's play, the tragic hero Hamlet thinks deeply about the meaning of life – and death.

People still celebrate Viking festivals. For example, in the Shetland Isles, where many Vikings settled, people celebrate 'Up-Helly-Aa' on the last Tuesday in January. This marks the end of Yule, the Viking mid-winter festival. They dress up as Vikings, parade through the streets, then burn a lifesize model of a Viking warship.

170 **Father Christmas was originally a Viking god.** Yule (mid-winter) was one of the most important Viking festivals. It was a time when Vikings held feasts and exchanged presents. They also believed that Viking gods travelled across the sky, bringing good things – just like Father Christmas!

▶ Today, as in Viking times, the light and warmth of blazing fires at mid-winter festivals bring hope and cheerfulness at a cold, dark time.

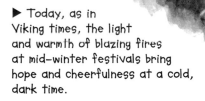

▲ This modern picture of Father Christmas shows him riding through the sky in a Viking-style sleigh, pulled by reindeer from Viking lands.

SAMURAI

171 **For hundreds of years, there was a group of warriors in Japan known as samurai.** Their name means 'someone who serves'. All samurai served a warlord (military leader) and battles were fought between armies of rival warlords. Samurai followed a set of rules called *bushido*. These rules told them how to behave, not just in battle, but in everyday life. Respected members of Japanese society, the bravest and fiercest samurai became well-known figures.

▼ Samurai armies fought at close range, on foot and on horseback. This scene shows the Battle of Kawanakajima in 1561, in the north of the main Japanese island of Honshu.

From emperor to shogun

172 Japan is an island country in the Pacific Ocean, located off the coast of mainland Asia. It is made up of four main islands (Hokkaido, Honshu, Shikoku and Kyushu) and nearly 4000 smaller ones. The islands are mountainous, with forested slopes and fast-flowing rivers. There are many active volcanoes, including the famous Mount Fuji.

▲ Jimmu, the first in a long line of emperors who ruled Japan.

Kyoto

Osaka

Tok

Nara

SHIKOKU

KYUSHU

▲ Japan is a nation of many islands that lie close together. It has had several capital cities over the years.

QUIZ

1. Which family took power away from the emperor?
2. Who was the first emperor of Japan?
3. What is the name of Japan's most famous volcano?
4. Which was the first permanent capital of Japan?

Answers:
1. The Fujiwara family
2. Jimmu 3. Mount Fuji 4. Nara

173 Japan was once ruled by emperors. Legend says that the first emperor was Jimmu, who reigned in 660 BC. Early emperors had great power. Then about AD 800 they became 'figurehead rulers'. This meant that they were still heads of state, but had little power.

DATE	PERIOD	NOTABLE EVENTS
14,000–300 BC	Jomon	• Early people are hunter-gatherers and decorate clay pottery with distinctive patterns
300 BC–AD 300	Yayoi	• Farmers begin to grow rice in paddy fields
AD 300–710	Kofun	• Buddhism is introduced to Japan
AD 710–794	Nara	• Nara becomes the first permanent capital city
794–1185	Heian	• Kyoto becomes the capital city
1185–1333	Kamakura	• Battle of Dan-no-Ura • Minamoto Yoritomo becomes the first shogun
1333–1573	Muromachi	• Members of Ashikaga family become shoguns. They are finally driven out by the warlord Oda Nobunaga
1573–1603	Azuchi-Momoyama	• Oda Nobunaga is succeeded by Toyotomi Hideyoshie • Japan is reunited
1603–1868	Edo	• Japan isolates itself from the rest of the world • US Commodore Matthew Perry forces the Japanese government to open up ports for trade
1868–1912	Meiji	• Japan becomes modernized and grows to be a world power

HOKKAIDO

HONSHU

▶ Japanese history is divided into several periods. These are often named after the most powerful family, or the site of the capital city at that time.

174
In about AD 800, power was taken from the emperor. It fell into the hands of the Fujiwara clan. They were a noble family that had married into royalty, and for about 300 years they were the real rulers of Japan. However in the 1100s, the Fujiwaras lost control after a bitter war. From then on, power passed to military dictators called shoguns.

175
Shogun means 'commander of the forces'. He was a military dictator – the person in control, with unlimited power. In 1192, Minamoto Yoritomo became the first shogun. He was known as the 'barbarian-conquering great general'.

▶ Minamoto Yoritomo, the first shogun. Shoguns controlled Japan until 1867.

176
Japan's first permanent capital city was Nara, on the island of Honshu. It became capital in AD 710 and the emperor lived there. In AD 794, Kyoto was made the new capital and home of the emperor. Tokyo, which was known as Edo until 1868, is now the present-day capital.

Religion and ritual

177 **Japanese society was divided between rich and poor.** A few rich families owned all the land and the poor owned none. The poorest people worked on the land, and had to pay taxes to the powerful landowners. This type of system is known as feudalism. Japan was a feudal society for hundreds of years.

▶ At the top of Japanese society was the emperor, even though he had no real power. Merchants were the lowest class.

Figurehead

Emperor

Shogun
(Political leader)

Daimyos
(Warlords)

Samurai
(Warriors)

Ronin
(Paid soldiers)

Peasants
(Farmers and fishermen)

Artisans
(Craftspeople)

Merchants
(Sales people)

Warrior class

90 percent of the population

Lowest class

▶ There are many statues of Buddha in Japan. This one is made of bronze and is 800 years old.

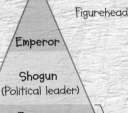

178 **The two main Japanese religions are Shinto and Buddhism.** Shinto is an ancient religion in which the emperor is said to be a descendant of the Sun god. Its followers believe that spirits inhabit trees, waterfalls and other natural things. Buddhism is founded on the teachings of Siddhartha Gautama. He was called the Buddha and lived in India in the 4th or 5th century BC.

◀ Shinto priests bang drums during ceremonies. The sound is believed to attract the gods' attention.

180

Before battle, a samurai warrior might visit a Shinto shrine. A priest would give him a small cup of *sake* (rice wine) to drink, and the soldier would offer prayers to a god. In return for his prayers, the soldier hoped the god would protect him. Samurai had favourite gods to pray to, such as Taira Masakado (see pages 88–89). After he died, in AD 940, he was believed to have become a god.

◄ Shinto shrines were important places of worship. Samurai visited them to pray for good fortune.

179

Ancestors were special. If a samurai had heroes among his ancestors, he showed them great respect by displaying their names at his family altar. It was a way of keeping their memories alive, and the warrior hoped he would inherit their bravery and courage.

181

Rituals were very important. These were set ways of doing ordinary things. During the 1400s, samurai began to carry out the tea ceremony. This was an elaborate way of making and enjoying a cup of tea. The tea was made by carrying out steps in a precise order.

▼ Equipment used during the tea ceremony. The ritual is linked to Buddhist ideas of tranquility (calmness).

Hishaku (water ladle)

Kama (iron pot used to heat the water)

Mizusashi (container containing cold water)

Chashaku (tea scoop)

Chasen (bamboo whisk)

Chaki (dry tea leaf container)

Chawan (tea bowl, used for drinking)

The first samurai

182 The first samurai appeared in the AD 900s. They were warriors who belonged to the private armies of Japan's noble families, or clans. The clans owned large amounts of land, which they needed to protect from their rivals. The best way to do that was to build up an army of soldiers in case of battle.

183 Samurai protected their bodies with armour. The first samurai wore armour made from small iron or leather scales, laced together with silk or leather cords. The scales were arranged into separate sections, each of which was designed to protect a different part of the samurai's body.

▶ A samurai warrior of the AD 900s. Mounted warriors were especially skilled at using the bow and arrow.

184 In the early years of the samurai, the soldier on horseback was the elite warrior. He was an archer, and fired arrows from a bow as his horse galloped along at speed. The mounted archer practised his archery techniques over and over again. In battle, when he had fired all his arrows, an archer fought with a sword.

Bow

Armoured sleeve

Shin guard

Shoulder guard

Arrows

Armoured kilt

Sword

185 Infantry (foot soldiers) were lower class fighters. It was their job to hold up their shields to protect the mounted archers, who were seen as the main fighting force. As well as defending the horsemen, the infantry were also responsible for disrupting the enemy by setting fire to their property.

Minamoto clan *mon*, a flower

Taira clan *mon*, a butterfly

▲ ▶ Each clan had its own *mon*, or family crest. It was used on flags, and helped soldiers to identify their comrades.

186 The two leading clans were the Minamoto (also called the Genji) and the Taira (also called the Heike). They were bitter rivals whose armies fought battles against each other to decide which was the leading clan.

Let battle begin!

▼ Battles began with archers firing a volley of whistling arrows.

187 **An argument between rival clans would often lead to a battle.** When the two sides faced each other on the battlefield, the armies followed a strict sequence of events. The battle began with archers firing arrows that made a whistling sound. The noise was believed to be a sign to the gods, asking them to protect the samurai who were about to fight. It was also a scary sound for the enemy.

188 **It was an honour to be first into battle.** A man was chosen from among the mounted warriors. He was picked because he was a champion fighter and came from a long line of warriors. Facing the enemy, he named his ancestors and listed his achievements in battle. It was a challenge to the other side to send out a warrior of equal status.

189 An opponent from the rival army would ride out to meet his enemy. The two men then fought a duel on horseback, firing arrows at each other as they rode at speed around the battlefield. It was a contest to show who was the best rider and the best archer.

190 If the archery duel didn't produce a winner, the two men began hand-to-hand combat. They dismounted from their horses, and fought until one of them was killed. The winner cut off his opponent's head and presented it to his commander as proof of his courage and skill. After the duel, fighting broke out. Men fought one to one, in groups, on horseback and on foot.

▲ In hand-to-hand fighting, samurai fought with swords that had long, curved blades.

I DON'T BELIEVE IT!

The mounted archer Minamoto Tametomo described how his arrow went straight through his opponent's saddle, passed through his body, then came out the other side!

191 The element of surprise was one of the most effective fighting tactics. Soldiers would try to catch their enemies off-guard and ambush them, or creep up to their buildings and set them on fire.

Taira Masakado

192 Born around AD 903, Taira Masakado is the first samurai commander that historians know much about. Part of the Taira clan, Masakado was the great-great grandson of Emperor Kammu. In his youth he served at the court of the Fujiwara clan in the capital Kyoto. The Fujiwaras were Japan's rulers at the time.

▼ Taira Masakado knocks a foot soldier to the ground. In old pictures such as this, he is always shown as a brave warrior.

193 The Taira clan had its origins in AD 825, when the surname Taira was given to a branch of the royal family. The Taira settled in Hitachi, a district northwest of present-day Tokyo. They became the ruling family of the region, and built up a private army.

194 Masakado wanted the Fujiwaras to appoint him as head of the national police. The Fujiwara clan refused to do this, so Masakado left their court and moved to the Kanto district of central Japan. From there, he led a war against the Fujiwara clan. In AD 939 he conquered districts in eastern Japan, and proclaimed himself to be the new emperor.

195

The government sent an army to defeat Masakado, who they regarded as a rebel. This army was led by Taira Sadamori. The two sides clashed at the Battle of Kojima, in AD 940, and Masakado was killed in the fighting. His head was cut off and sent to the emperor in Kyoto as proof of his death.

▼ The Battle of Kojima took place during a gale. Wooden shields erected by Masakado's army were blown down.

196

In Kyoto, Masakado's head was put on a platform. Legend says the head flew back to Masakado's base in Kanto. From there it went on to Shibasaki, where it was buried with honour. Today, that place is known as Masakado Kubizuka (the Hill of Masakado's head), in Tokyo. Masakado is seen as a hero who fought the government for the rights of ordinary people.

▼ At the Hill of Masakado's Head, there is a shrine in honour of Taira Masakado.

Minamoto Yoshiie

197 The Minamoto clan was an offshoot of the Japanese royal family. But in the AD 800s it was decided that none of them would be emperor. They were given the surname Minamoto and moved from the capital at Kyoto to a new base at Osaka, in southern Japan. Here they became the district's ruling family.

198 Minamoto Yoshiie was a samurai commander. He turned the Minamoto clan into a major fighting force. Born in 1039, at Kawachi, in the district of Osaka, his father was a samurai leader, and Yoshiie learned all the skills of the warrior from him.

◄ Minamoto Yoshiie was one of the greatest samurai commanders.

▶ Yoshiie earned the title *Hachiman-Taro*, meaning 'son of the god of war'.

199 Yoshiie's first battles were against the Abe clan. He fought alongside his father to defeat them in a war that raged for about nine years, and ended in 1062. The Minamoto clan took control of much of north Japan, with Yoshiie as ruler. Twenty years later, he defeated the Kiyowara clan, who had started to challenge him. The Minamotos were the undisputed rulers of north Japan.

I DON'T BELIEVE IT!

Once, Yoshiie guessed that his enemy was about to ambush him in a surprise attack because he saw a flock of geese suddenly fly out of a forest.

200 After each battle, Yoshiie spoke to his troops. Men who had shown the most courage were invited to sit on a 'bravery' seat. All of them wanted this honour. No one wanted to sit on the other 'cowardice' seat. To be called a coward was a disgrace.

▼ A bronze statue of Minamoto Yoshiie in Fukushima, on the island of Honshu.

201 Yoshiie's victories made him the greatest general in Japan. He made Kyoto his home, and he hoped the government would reward him with a position of power, but they never did. Yoshiie spent his last years living quietly in the capital, where he died in 1106.

The Gempei War

202 **As Japan's clans became stronger, a power struggle began.** The greatest conflict was between the Taira and Minamoto clans, who clashed in a series of battles known as the Gempei War, fought between 1180 and 1185. Both clans were related to Japan's royal family, and they wanted to control it – and the rest of Japan.

203 **The Gempei War began when Taira Kiyomori ordered the death of Minamoto Yoritomo.** Kiyomori and Yoritomo were the leaders of their respective clans. At first, the Taira forces were successful, and Yoritomo's army was heavily defeated. But the war was not over.

▶ Minamoto Yoritomo (1147–1199) led the Minamoto clan during the Gempei War.

▼ In 1180, Minamoto Yoritomo sent one of his men to kill an enemy from the Taira clan. This marked the start of the Gempei War.

204 **The Taira clan had a reputation for being harsh.** As the war progressed, Taira troops started to defect and join the Minamoto army. It was now the Minamoto's turn for battle honours. In 1183, the Minamoto army seized the capital at Kyoto, then attacked the last strongholds of Taira resistance, which were in western Japan.

SAMURAI SYMBOLS

Every samurai clan had its own *mon* (see page 85). This was a symbol that was easy to recognize. *Mons* were usually based on plants or simple patterns made from dots, curves and lines. Some were based on animals, but these were less common. What *mon* would you design for your family? Look at the *mons* in the pictures in this book to give you some ideas.

205

The final action of the Gempei War was the sea battle of Dan-no-ura, in 1185. Warships of the Taira and Minamoto clans fought in the narrow strip of water between the islands of Honshu and Kyushu. When it was clear the Minamoto would win, many of the Taira threw themselves into the sea.

206

By 1192, the Minamoto clan controlled Japan. That year, Minamoto Yoritomo visited the emperor in Kyoto. The emperor appointed him as the first shogun (military dictator). From then on, Japan had two rulers – the god-like emperor (who had little power) and the shogun, the most powerful person in the land. It was a system that lasted until the mid-1800s.

▼ The Taira clan were defeated at the Battle of Dan-no-ura. This scene shows Taira Tomomori tied to an anchor, about to drown himself.

Bushido – the samurai code

207 Samurai followed a code of behaviour known as bushido. It means 'the way of the warrior'. *Bushido* was a set of rules that governed all aspects of a samurai's lifestyle. It demonstrated that a samurai was an educated and refined man with knowledge of the arts and literature – as well as being a brutal killer who would slice off his enemy's head without hesitation.

▼ As well as being fierce warriors, samurai were required to be well dressed and educated.

208 A samurai was expected to be a confident warrior. He had to believe he was strong, not just hope that he was. Self-belief was a key part of *bushido*. If warriors had doubts in themselves it meant they were weak, and weakness was not 'the way of the warrior'.

◄ A samurai was expected to show confidence at all times, and believe he was a worthy warrior.

SAMURAI

◄ This samurai is bowing to his master, showing he is loyal and obedient, a key part of *bushido*.

210 Courage was one of the most important rules of *bushido*. To show courage, a samurai had to demonstrate that he was prepared to fight to the death. If he was outnumbered in battle, he had to carry on fighting. Running away was a sign of cowardice, which was punished.

209 Showing loyalty to the warlord was another rule of *bushido*. The warlord gave orders, and samurai obeyed them without question. By obeying orders, a samurai showed obedience.

I DON'T BELIEVE IT!
Samurai were told to be careful when chasing their enemies. If an enemy got too far ahead, he could easily turn around and charge, putting the attacking samurai in danger.

211 If a samurai made a big mistake, he was punished under the rules of *bushido*. In the most serious cases, he would kill himself. This was called *seppuku*, or *hara-kiri*. The samurai first ate a meal. After this he opened up his robes and plunged a dagger into his stomach. As he did this, another samurai cut his head off with a swing of his sword.

◄ A samurai about to commit *seppuku*, cutting open his own stomach.

Samurai armies

212 By the 1550s, Japan was divided into many states, each of which was ruled by a daimyo. He was the warlord and head of a clan. Rival clans were almost constantly at war with each other. To protect their territory, warlords had large armies. As fighting increased, the armies grew more organized.

214 Foot soldiers were called *ashigaru*. They made up a large part of a warlord's army, and there were always many more *ashigaru* than mounted samurai. *Ashigaru* fought with swords, spears, bows and *naginata* (see page 101). From the 1540s they began to use guns called arquebuses.

213 Armies clashed during the fighting season, which lasted from spring until the end of summer. No fighting took place during the harvest season, which began in September, or in winter. Most foot soldiers were peasants from farming communities, and when it was harvest time they returned to their homes to gather crops.

215 A samurai army was divided into units of men. The elite troops were always the men on horseback. The *ashigaru* were organized into groups of spearmen, archers and arquebusiers (soldiers with firearms). Other groups of *ashigaru* carried flags and banners, and some were given the job of carrying the army's baggage.

216 On the battlefield, generals controlled troop movements by waving fans. The fans had swinging tassels on them, making the fan movements easy to see. Sound signals were another way of sending information to the troops, such as blowing on conch shells and beating on drums and gongs.

▼ A samurai army on the march. *Ashigaru* foot soldiers are flanked by mounted samurai. The most powerful clans had armies of over 100,000 men.

Warrior training

217 Boys were taught to be warriors. They began school at about the age of seven, and for the next five or six years were taught to read, write and play musical instruments. From about the age of ten, they were taught to fight. When a boy reached 13, he had a coming-of-age ceremony, and from then on he was ready to fight in battle.

▶ Boys were taught to fight using sticks, but these would eventually be replaced with swords.

218 Some clans set up military training schools, or *dojo*. Here, boys were taught martial arts by trainers, or *sensei*. The *sensei* were skilled in the use of weapons, and had served in samurai armies. It was their job to pass these essential skills on.

I DON'T BELIEVE IT

Left-handed children born to samurai families had their left arms tied up, forcing them to become right-handed.

219 Mounted warriors were the elite troops of a warlord's army. Their main weapon was the bow, and they had to fire arrows at moving targets as their horses raced at speed. They practised by firing arrows at running dogs. At the start of training, most arrows missed, but eventually they would learn when to release an arrow to hit a moving target.

221 Women married to samurai were trained to fight. Although their main work was to look after the family, there was always a chance that an enemy raiding party might attack the family home. To fight off attackers, women used daggers and *naginata* (see page 101). Some warlords had bands of armed women patrolling the grounds of their castles.

▲ When using dogs as target practice, the horsemen used blunt arrows. It was not their intention to kill the dogs.

220 In another type of target practice, mounted samurai fired arrows at targets fixed to poles. They rode along a course, and as they moved past a small wooden board they fired an arrow. There were three targets, and the archer only had three arrows. The most skilful samurai made each arrow count and hit each target.

▶ Tomoe Gozen (c. 1157–1247) was a female warrior who fought on the side of the Minamoto clan during the Gempei War.

Weapons with edges

Hilt or handle
(*tsuka*)

222 Swords were the main edged weapons used by samurai. The blades were made of steel, in a process that involved heating and folding the metal several times. A sword was seen as the 'soul' of a samurai. The finest swords were made by master swordsmiths. They carved their own names, and the names of the owners, along with good luck verses on the sword handles.

223 New swords were tested for sharpness. They were tried out on sheaves of straw wrapped around bamboo, oak poles, copper plates and even metal helmets. Sometimes they were tested on people too, and were used to behead criminals. The best swords were so sharp they could cut through several bodies placed on top of one another.

▶ A master swordsmith at work. Each time the steel was reshaped, the sword became stronger.

Scabbard (*saya*)

Guard (*tsuba*)

Point of blade (*kissaki*)

224

The main fighting sword was called a *katana*. It had a long, curving blade and was mainly used for combat on foot. The samurai held his sword in both hands as he moved it in a series of attacking strokes, from zigzags and circles to up, down and diagonal slashes. He could also use it on horseback, holding it with one hand, not two.

▲ Each *katana* was highly prized. The best swords were given names, such as 'The Monster Cutter' or 'Little Dragon'.

▲ Guards at the end of the hilt (handle) of a *katana* stopped the swordsman's hand from slipping onto the blade.

225

Short swords called *tanto* were used for fighting at close quarters. Every samurai carried a *tanto*. It was often the stabbing thrust of a *tanto* that decided the outcome of a duel. The victorious samurai then cut off the loser's head.

▲ A short sword or *tanto* and its scabbard. Like the *katana*, the *tanto* was incredibly sharp.

◄ The curved blade at the end of a *naginata*.

226

Samurai used other weapons with sharp edges. The *naginata* was a long pole with a curved metal blade at the end. The blade was used for slashing, and the pole for beating. It was mainly a weapon of the *ashigaru*, who also used stabbing spears.

► Most spears had pointed tips. Some were hook-shaped and used to drag men from their horses.

Missile weapons

227 **The bow was as important to the samurai as the sword.** It was called a yumi, and was almost 2.5 metres in length. Made from strips of wood and bamboo, it fired arrows to a distance of about 380 metres, but its killing range was no more than about 80 metres.

▶ Arrowheads came in different shapes and sizes to carry out different functions.

Armour-piercing arrowheads

228 **Arrows were made of bamboo, and there were many types of arrowhead.** Some made whistling noises, some had armour-piercing tips, and some had forked heads to cut through ropes. One legend says a samurai archer sank an enemy ship by firing an arrow through its hull below the waterline.

Whistling arrowhead

Forked arrowhead

Match (rope for burning)

◀ The longbow was an effective weapon, and samurai archers were highly trained.

229
In siege warfare (attacking a castle or city), samurai armies used machines to hurl stones. The first stone-throwers were giant crossbows but these were eventually replaced by trebuchets, a type of catapult. Trebuchets were used to bombard enemies with heavy rocks, which shattered when they hit the ground, causing casualties and damage.

▼ Samurai soldiers prepare to hurl a rock from a trebuchet.

▼ An *ashigaru* takes aim with an arquebus. Although these guns fired bullets in quick succession, they were less accurate than a skilled archer using a bow.

Barrel

230
In the 1540s a new weapon arrived in Japan. It was the arquebus, a type of musket (a forerunner of the rifle). The Japanese called it a teppo, and it was carried by a foot soldier (ashigaru). The arquebus used gunpowder to fire a lead ball over a distance of about 500 metres, with a killing range of about 200 metres.

231
Another gunpowder weapon was the cannon. However, unlike the arquebus, which was widely used, the cannon was not very popular with samurai armies. Any cannons that were used came from Dutch and English ships that visited Japan.

◄ This soldier is using a large bore arquebus, which fired a big lead ball.

Amazing armour

① Shin guards
② Breeches
③ Armoured sleeves
④ Body armour
⑤ Shoulder guards
⑥ Neck guard
⑦ Head cloth
⑧ Face mask
⑨ Helmet

◄ Putting on armour was a complicated process with many stages.

232 **All samurai wore armour.** By the 1500s a standard type was in widespread use. It was made from small leather or metal scales sewn onto cloth. As each piece of armour was put on, it was laced to the next piece, until the samurai was securely tied into his armour.

233 **A samurai helmet was called a *kabuto*.** Before putting on a helmet, a samurai combed his hair back and wrapped a cloth around his head to form a padded area. Helmets were heavy, and to stop them falling off, samurai tied them under their chins.

▼ Helmets were made from several metal plates They were very ornate pieces of armour.

c. 1580

Early 17th century

18th century

234 Most samurai went into battle barefaced, but some wore a face mask, or *mempo*. This could cover the whole of the face, or just the chin, cheeks, mouth and nose. The mask was usually painted, and the mouth was shaped like a grimace so the warrior looked as if he was snarling.

▲ Some masks had bristling fake moustaches to make the wearer seem even more terrifying.

235 Samurai armour could be brightly coloured. Lacquer (varnish) was painted over each piece. It not only made the armour stand out, it also made it hard-wearing. The five 'lucky' colours were red, blue, yellow, black and white.

► Eighteenth century armour from the Edo Period.

236 Samurai of the Li clan in the 1500s were known as the Red Devils. Their armour was coated with red lacquer, making them instantly recognizable. They chose red to make themselves appear more frightening, and because no other clan wore this colour.

Helmet

Face mask

Neck guard

Shoulder guard

Cuirass (body armour)

Armoured sleeves

Armoured kilt

Greaves (leg armour)

Clothes and food

237 **For everyday clothing a samurai wore a *kimono*.** This was a long, wide-sleeved gown that came down to below his knees and was kept in place by a belt wrapped around the waist. He wore a pair of *hakama* (wide trousers) under the *kimono* and socks and sandals on his feet. His *katana* (sword) was tucked into his belt.

Kimono

Katana

▶ A samurai in everyday dress. Even though he was not fighting, he still carried his sword.

Hakama

◀ A samurai with a typically shaven head. His remaining hair was tied in a bun at the back.

Socks and sandals

238 **Tidy hair was important.** It was considered a disgrace if a man let his hair become untidy. In the 1500s, samurai began shaving the hair from the front part of their heads. This made it more comfortable to wear a helmet in battle. Hair at the sides and rear of the head was combed back and tied into a bun.

I DON'T BELIEVE IT!
Tokugawa Ieyasu, leader of the Tokugawa clan in the 1500s, didn't like shaved heads – he said it spoiled the look of a head when it was cut off!

239

Rice was the staple food in Japan. It was eaten boiled and steamed, and as rice cakes and rice balls. Fish, pork, boar and rabbit were the main meats eaten. When samurai went to war, most warriors took portions of rice with them. If they raided an enemy camp or village, they took the enemy's food supplies.

◀ A local farmer offers a samurai commander baskets of melons for his troops. Fruit was popular with soldiers on campaign.

240

Before a battle, samurai shared a meal together. It was a way of bringing the warriors closer to each other in the last few hours before fighting began.

241

A helmet was not just for wearing. Some foot soldiers (*ashigaru*) used their metal helmets as cooking pots! They turned them upside down and boiled rice inside them over a fire. Small groups of men probably took it in turns to cook for their comrades.

▶ An *ashigaru's* metal helmet had two functions – protective armour and a cooking pot to boil rice.

Castle fortresses

242 To protect their territory, samurai clans built castles. Some were built on flat plains, but most were built on mountains. Their purpose was to defend key areas such as bridges, river crossings, roads and mountain passes.

▶ A castle was surrounded by a strong wall. Inside were courtyards, each of which could be closed off if intruders broke through the main defences.

243 Castles built in the 1500s were heavily defended. At the centre was the keep – the tallest and grandest building within the castle grounds, where the *daimyo* (warlord) lived. If intruders broke through the castle's outer line of defence, they were faced by a series of walls with gates that took them into open courtyards – where they could be easily attacked.

I DON'T BELIEVE IT!

Tottori Castle was besieged for 200 days. The occupants ran out of food and had to eat grass, dead horses, and possibly even each other.

③

④

244 A clan's most important castle was the home of the *daimyo*. Around this castle were the homes of generals and family members. The more important the person was, the closer to the leader's castle they were allowed to live. A town grew up around the castle. Rice was grown in the surrounding fields to provide food for the townspeople.

245 Matsumoto Castle is one of Japan's finest samurai castles. It was built in the late 1500s, on a flat plain in central Japan. Its location made it an easy target, but the builders protected it with three moats and strong ramparts. The castle complex was surrounded by an earth wall 3.5 kilometres in circumference. The only way to enter or leave was through two heavily fortified gates.

246 Castles were difficult to attack. Armies besieged a castle until its occupants surrendered. When Takamatsu Castle was besieged in 1582, the attackers diverted a river until it formed a lake. As the lake grew, it flooded the castle, and the occupants gave in. The defeated leader rowed out on the lake and committed suicide (*seppuku*).

KEY
1. Keep (where the *daimyo* lived)
2. Moat
3. Outer wall
4. Inner wall
5. Gatehouse

The age of battles

247 Many battles took place all over Japan in the years 1450–1600. This time is known as the Warring States Period. It was a time of civil war, when rival states attacked each other, trying to win territory. The battles were fought on a large scale, and from the mid-16th century arquebuses were used – the first time this deadly firearm was put into practise in a big way.

248 Armies fought in battle formations. Generals decided which formation was best to use, and the troops moved into place. Formations had names such as 'birds in flight', 'keyhole' and 'half moon'. In the 'birds in flight' formation, the arquebusiers protected the archers, who fired arrows over the heads of the musketmen. The general was at the centre, surrounded by his warriors.

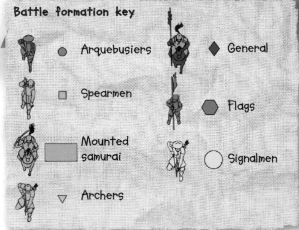

Battle formation key

● Arquebusiers ◆ General
□ Spearmen ⬡ Flags
▬ Mounted samurai ◯ Signalmen
▽ Archers

Birds in flight formation

▼ Three different types of battle formation. Every man knew his place and was expected to keep to it.

Keyhole formation

Half moon formation

249 The 'arrowhead' formation was used to break through enemy lines. Arquebusiers fired their muskets, opening up gaps in the enemy's front ranks. When the gaps were big enough, samurai rushed past their gunmen, and through the gaps. Hand-to-hand fighting followed using swords, daggers, *naginata* and spears.

◀ The arrowhead formation takes its name from the pointed arrow–like position of the troops.

250 After the battle, the victors took the spoils. The dead of both sides were stripped of their weapons and armour. Scavengers from nearby villages helped themselves to whatever they could carry. Wounded warriors were of no use to anyone. They were killed by local villagers, who then took their belongings.

251 The greatest prizes were the heads of the losers. They were cut off and presented to the general for him to inspect. First, the heads were washed, the hair was combed, and they were placed on spikes on boards. Labels attached to the hair gave the names of the dead, and the names of the men who had killed them.

▼ The severed head of an enemy soldier being presented for inspection.

I DON'T BELIEVE IT!
If the eyes of a severed head were closed, it was a lucky sign. If they were open and looking upwards, it was an unlucky sign.

Oda Nobunaga

252 One of greatest samurai commanders of the Warring States Period was Oda Nobunaga. He was born in 1534, and became *daimyo* (warlord) of the Oda clan when he was just 16. Because he was so young, rival clans thought they could easily overpower his army and take his land – but they were wrong. In a series of battles, Nobunaga's forces defeated his enemies.

253 Nobunaga's rise to power began in 1560. In that year, his territory was invaded by the Imagawa clan. The Imagawa army was 12 times the size of Nobunaga's, and they quickly took several of his fortresses. It looked as if Nobunaga would be defeated. But, during a thunderstorm, Nobunaga mounted a surprise attack. The Imagawa *daimyo* was killed, and Nobunaga's territory was saved.

▶ Japanese artists portrayed Oda Nobunaga as a fearsome warrior.

254 The Battle of Nagashino was fought in 1575. In this great battle, Nobunaga sent an army to the castle of Nagashino. The castle was besieged by an army from the Takeda clan. Nobunaga's plan was to end the siege by fighting the Takedas.

255
The Nobunaga and Takeda armies clashed on a plain near Nagashino Castle. Mounted samurai from the Takeda clan charged at Nobunaga's forces, and were felled by shots from as many as 3000 arquebusiers. A second wave of Takeda horsemen swooped down, by which time the musketmen had reloaded. After hours of bitter fighting, the Takeda army withdrew.

▼ A scene from *Kagemusha*, a film released in 1980. Set during the Warring States Period, it ends with the Battle of Nagashino.

256
Oda Nobunaga died in 1582. He had become the most powerful general in Japan, and acted as if he was the country's shogun. This made him many enemies. On a visit to Honnoji Temple, in Kyoto, he was attacked by his own men. Some accounts say he died in the attack, others say he was captured and forced to commit *seppuku*.

Flags and standards

257 Samurai carried flags and standards into battle. There could be hundreds of flags fluttering in the wind on the battlefield, and each one had its own meaning. Some were decorated with family, clan or religious symbols, others had messages on them. It was the job of an army's foot soldiers to carry the flags.

▲ The Soma-Nomaoi Festival is held each year in Haramachi City. Here, horsemen in traditional samurai armour parade with flags decorated with clan symbols, or *mons*.

258 A battlefield could be a confusing place. In the rush of horses and the scattering of men, it was easy for a soldier to become separated from his fellow warriors, or lose sight of his *daimyo* (warlord). If this happened, all he had to do was look around for the flags of his own side, which he would recognize by their familiar symbols.

▼ ▶ The red umbrella great standard of Oda Nobunaga and the golden bell great standard of Mukai Tadakatsu, leader of the Omura clan.

259 In samurai battles of the late 1500s and 1600s, the daimyo had two standards. They were the 'great standard' and the 'lesser standard', both mounted on long poles. A standard was an important object to a clan. Not only was it instantly recognizable, it represented what the clan stood for, and was to be protected.

261

Samurai could attach flags to their backs. These were called *sashimono*. The shaft of the flag slotted into a holder in the armour, leaving both hands free for weapons. *Sashimono* were often decorated with the clan's colours or symbols. Some samurai painted their flags with messages, giving the name of the wearer and the name of the man he hoped to kill in battle.

▶ A *sashimono* attached to the back of a samurai. 'Leader' is written on his flag in Japanese.

260

It was a great honour to be a standard-bearer, but this honour brought danger. The enemy was drawn towards the other side's standard, so the standard-bearer was always in the thick of the fighting. The defending army would do everything they could to save the standard from being captured. If the standard-bearer fell, another man quickly took his place.

DESIGN A FLAG

Have a close look at the flags pictured in this book, then design one of your own. Note how the flags are long and thin, which made them easy to carry. Keep your design simple and bold, and use strong colours so that it really stands out.

Samurai in decline

◀ Tokugawa Ieyasu, the shogun who brought a long period of peace to Japan.

262 On 21 October 1600, the Battle of Sekigahara took place. It was fought between the armies of Tokugawa Ieyasu (with 80,000 men) and Ishida Mitsunari (100,000 men). An estimated 30,000 men died on the battlefield. The Tokugawa clan won, and the battle brought an end to the Warring States Period.

263 Tokugawa Ieyasu became shogun in 1603. It was the start of a relatively peaceful period in Japan's history that lasted for the next 250 years. In 1639, Japan became a 'closed country'. It was forbidden to have contact with foreigners, and Japanese people were not even allowed to leave the country.

▼ The arrival of the American navy in Tokyo harbour in 1853 caused great concern in Japan.

▼ Emperor Meiji ruled Japan from 1868 to 1912.

264 The clans were now at peace with each other, and their armies were disbanded. The idea of going to war to steal another clan's territory became a thing of the past. Samurai traditions and rituals still carried on, but they were performed for peaceful purposes.

265 In 1853 and 1854, a fleet of ships from the USA arrived in Tokyo Harbour. The American fleet was led by Commodore Matthew Perry. His aim was for Japan to stop being a closed country and to open up to foreign trade. The Tokugawa clan were still Japan's rulers, and the shogun Tokugawa Iesada decided to open up the country. Many Japanese thought this was a bad thing.

266 Japan's system of an emperor sharing power with the shogun came to an end in 1867. It was a system that had lasted for 675 years. The last shogun, Tokugawa Yoshinobu, handed power back in 1867, and in 1868, Emperor Meiji became the sole ruler of Japan. For some people, these changes were too much to bear.

The last samurai

267 **The Satsuma Rebellion took place in 1877.** Samurai were unhappy at the changes in Japan. For centuries they had been respected, and feared, members of society. Gradually their way of living had changed, and now they felt out of place as Japan began a process of modernization, bringing to an end centuries of feudal rule. When they were told to lay down their swords, it was the final insult, and a rebellion began.

▲ Soldiers of the Japanese army with rifles (left) clash with samurai armed with *naginata*.

▶ Saigo Takamori (1828–1877), leader of the rebel forces during the Satsuma Rebellion, was the last samurai commander.

268 **Leader of the rebellion was Saigo Takamori.** His army of 40,000 samurai fought against a larger government force. The samurai fought with their traditional weapons – the sword and the bow. The Japanese army fought with rifles.

269 **The rebellion lasted for about eight months.** It ended at the Battle of Shiroyama, on 24 September 1877. Takamori's forces had been reduced to a few hundred men. He was heavily outnumbered, but refused to surrender as this was against the *bushido* code. Takamori was wounded, and then he committed *seppuku* rather than face being captured. His remaining men were cut down by gunfire.

270 Many films have been made about the samurai. The most famous is *Seven Samurai*, made in Japan in 1954 and set in the Warring States Period. Another is *Kagemusha*, made in 1980. Both of these films were directed by Akira Kurosawa, who is regarded as the greatest samurai film-maker of all time. Hollywood has also made films about samurai, such as *The Last Samurai* in 2003 with Tom Cruise in the title role.

▼ In the 2003 Warner Brothers' film *The Last Samurai*, actor Tom Cruise plays the part of an American fighting on the side of the samurai during the Satsuma Rebellion.

I DON'T BELIEVE IT!

In the *Star Wars* movies, the costume of Darth Vader was inspired by samurai armour.

ARMS & ARMOUR

271 People have used arms and armour to hunt, defend themselves and attack other people for thousands of years. Arms are weapons that are carried by a single person. Armour is something that is worn or carried to protect against injury. Early armour was made from wood or leather, and the first arms were made from wood or stone.

▼ At the battle of Lechfeld in AD 955 the Germans crushed the much larger army of Magyars. The Germans succeeded because they were wearing suits of mail armour and carrying new weapons.

The first arms

272 Some of the first arms were made from stone. The earliest humans lived hundreds of thousands of years ago. Archaeologists (scientists who study the remains of ancient humans) have found weapons made of sharpened stone that were made by these ancient people.

▲ This hand axe is made from a single piece of stone. It was held in the hand and used with a chopping motion.

273 Early weapons were used for both hunting and fighting. Archaeologists have found bones from cattle, deer and mammoths, and discovered that these animals were hunted and killed by ancient people using stone weapons.

▶ Around 75,000 years ago, spears were made from a stone point, which was attached to a wooden handle with leather straps.

274 The first warriors did not use armour. It is thought that early tribes of people fought each other to get control of the best hunting grounds or sources of water. These men may not have used armour, relying instead on dodging out of the way of enemy weapons.

275

Shields were an early form of defence. A thrust from a spear could be stopped by holding a piece of wood in the way. People soon began to produce shields made of flat pieces of wood with a handle on the back. Over the years, shields came to be produced in many different shapes, and from a wide range of materials including metal, wood and leather.

▲ By about 300 BC, the Celts of Europe were producing beautiful shields decorated with bronze and colourful enamel. Some, like this one found in London, may have been used in ceremonies.

▶ Flint is a hard stone that can be chipped and flaked into a wide variety of shapes to produce different types of weapons, such as these points or tips for arrows.

276

Spears were the first effective weapons. Many early spears consisted of a stone point mounted on the end of a wooden pole. With a spear, a man could reach his enemy while still out of reach of the opponent's hand-held weapons. The earliest known spears are 400,000 years old and were found in Germany.

I DON'T BELIEVE IT!

The oldest signs of warfare come from Krapina, Croatia. Human bones over 120,000 years old have been found there that show marks caused by stone spearheads.

Ancient civilizations

277 **Early Egyptians may have used their hair as armour.** Some ancient Egyptians grew their hair very long, then plaited it thickly and wrapped it around their heads when going into battle. It is thought that this may have helped protect their heads.

▲ The Egyptian pharaoh Tutankhamun is shown firing a bow while riding in a chariot to attack the enemies of Egypt.

278 **Some Egyptian soldiers had shields that were as big as themselves.** Around 1800 BC, soldiers carried shields that were the height of a man. They hid behind their shields as the enemy attacked, then leapt out to use their spears.

279
Egyptian infantry (foot) soldiers often used axes. Soldiers that served as part of the bodyguard of the pharaoh (king) carried special axes. These weapons were made of bronze and each had a heavy round weight that meant they could deliver a heavier blow in battle.

▲ The curved blade of an Egyptian war axe. The weapon was able to crush any armour or shields in use at the time. This type of axe was used to cut, while other axes were used to pierce armour.

280
Assyrians wore long cloaks of mail. Some soldiers in the Assyrian army wore armour made entirely of mail around 900 BC. This was a series of interlocking metal rings that could withstand blows from swords or spears.

281
Babylonians wore armour that was brightly-coloured. Around 1000 BC, the ancient city of Babylon, Mesopotamia (now part of modern Iraq), was famous for its wealth. Babylonian soldiers wore armour that they often painted with bright colours to make themselves look more impressive in battle.

▶ An Assyrian army assaults a fortified city in Mesopotamia using siege towers and bows.

Hoplites and phalanxes

282 Hoplites were armoured infantry. From about 700 BC Greek infantry (foot soldiers) were equipped with a shield, helmet, spear and sword. They were called 'hoplites' ('armoured men'). Each hoplite used his own weapons and armour.

283 A Greek who lost his shield was a coward. The shield carried by hoplites was over one metre across and made of wood and bronze. It was very heavy, and anyone trying to run away from an enemy would throw it away, so men who lost their shields in battle were often accused of cowardice.

284 Hoplites fought in formations called phalanxes. When going into battle, hoplites stood shoulder to shoulder so that their shields overlapped, and pointed their spears forwards over the shields. A phalanx was made up of six or more ranks of hoplites, one behind the other.

▶ The success of Greek soldiers in battle depended on them keeping tightly in formation so that enemy soldiers could not get past the line of shields.

I DON'T BELIEVE IT!

Spartan hoplites were so tough that they reckoned they could easily win any battle, even if they were outnumbered by as many as five to one!

285
Greek spears had a 'lizard stabber'. Hoplite spears had a bronze spike at the bottom end. This was used to stick the spear upright into the ground and was called a 'sauroter', meaning 'lizard stabber'.

286
The best helmets were made from a single sheet of metal. Skilled metalworkers in the Greek city of Corinth invented a way to make a helmet by beating a single sheet of bronze into shape. This produced a helmet that was much stronger than one made of several pieces of metal. The helmets were called 'Corinthian'.

Roman legions

▲ A Roman legion marches out of a border fortress supervised by the legate, who commands the legion.

287 Armoured infantry formed the legions. The main fighting formation of the Roman army was the legion, a force of about 6000 men. Most were equipped with body armour, a helmet, a large rectangular shield, a sword and a throwing spear.

▶ The armour of a legionary was made up of several pieces, each of which could be replaced if it was damaged.

288 Roman armour was made of metal strips. At the height of the Roman Empire, around AD 50 to 250, legionaries wore armour called *lorica segmentata*. It was made up of strips of metal that were bent to fit the body, and held together by straps and buckles.

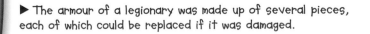

► In close combat, Roman soldiers used the gladius. It was a short sword, meant for stabbing rather than cutting.

291 Roman swords were copied from the Spanish. After 200 BC, Roman soldiers carried swords with straight blades and sharp points. They were copied from swords used by Spanish soldiers who defeated the Romans in battle.

► An auxiliary soldier wearing a short mail tunic and helmet, and carrying an oval shield. He has a gladius and javelin as weapons.

289 Roman auxiliaries wore cheaper armour. Every Roman legion included soldiers called auxiliaries (soldiers from places other than Rome). These units had to provide their own armour, often wearing tunics covered with mail or scale armour, which was made up of lots of small metal plates.

290 Roman shields could form a 'tortoise'. One tactic used by the Romans was called the 'testudo', or 'tortoise'. Soldiers formed short lines close together, holding their shields so they interlocked on all sides and overhead, just like the shell of a tortoise. In this formation they could advance on an enemy, safe from spears or arrows.

The Barbarians

292 Celts used chariots to intimidate the enemy. Battles between rival Celt tribes often began with famous warriors riding in chariots and performing tricks to show how skilled they were.

293 The Huns were lightly equipped. Around the year AD 370 the Huns swept into Europe from Asia. They fought on horseback with bows and spears, but wore no armour. They moved quickly, and showed no mercy.

294 The Dacian falx was a terrible weapon. The Dacians lived in what is now Romania around AD 400–600 and fought mostly on foot. Some Dacian warriors carried a long, curved sword with a broad blade that was called a falx. This weapon was so sharp and heavy that it could slice a person in half.

▶ The speed and accuracy of mounted Hun archers terrified the Romans.

295 The Franks were named after their favourite weapon. One tribe of Germans who lived around AD 300–600 were famous for using small throwing axes. These weapons had a short haft (handle) and a small, square-shaped head and were called 'francisca'. The men who used them were called franks, and soon the entire tribe took the name. They later gave the name to the country France.

◀ A Dacian warrior carrying a falx. Dacians were a people who lived outside the Roman Empire and often fought the Romans.

▼ A helmet belonging to an Anglo-Saxon king who ruled in East Anglia, England, about AD 625. It was made of iron and decorated with gold and silver.

296 Many barbarians wore armour decorated with gold, silver and precious stones. 'Barbarian' was the Roman name for uncivilized peoples outside the Roman Empire. They loved to show how rich they were and did this to emphasise their status within their tribe.

The Heavenly Kingdom

297 Chinese troops wore armour made of dozens of metal plates. The plates were about 8 centimetres by 6 centimetres and were sewn onto a leather garment or held together by leather thongs. Around 221 BC the various Chinese states were united. The Chinese believed this unity was the basis of their power and wealth.

298 Silk shirts helped protect against arrows. Many Chinese soldiers wore silk shirts under their armour. If an arrow pierced the armour it would drag the silk shirt into the wound without tearing it. By gently pulling on the shirt, the arrow could be extracted cleanly.

▼ A patrol of Chinese soldiers guarding the Great Wall around AD 200.

299

Crossbows were first used in China. They were more powerful than the bows used by nomadic tribesmen living north of China, so they were often used by troops manning the northern frontier. Crossbows consist of a short, powerful bow mounted on a wooden shaft and operated by a trigger.

300

Infantry used pole weapons. Chinese infantry often carried spears around 2 metres in length. Often an axelike chopping weapon, a slicing blade or a side spike replaced the spearhead. These weapons allowed the infantry to attack their enemies with a variety of actions to get around shields.

301

Chinese cavalry were heavily armed. When patrolling border regions, the Chinese cavalry operated in large formations that could defeat any tribal force causing trouble. The men were equipped with iron helmets and body armour, together with wooden shields and long lances tipped with iron.

QUIZ

1. In what year was China first united?
2. What did Chinese soldiers wear as protection against arrows?
3. Did the nomadic tribesmen live north or south of China?

Answers:
1. 221 BC 2. Silk shirts
3. North of China

The Dark Ages

302 The Dark Ages followed the fall of Rome in AD 410. Barbarian peoples took over the Western Roman Empire, and ancient culture and skills were lost. The Eastern Roman Empire lost power and lands to barbarians, but survived to become the Byzantine Empire. The Byzantines continued to use Roman-style arms and armour.

▲ English warriors patrol the great dyke built by King Offa of Mercia to define the border with Wales in AD 784.

303 English cavalry were lightly armed. Britain was invaded and settled by Germanic tribes from around AD 450, and by around AD 700 they ruled most of the island. Only the richest Englishmen wore body armour. Most went into battle armed with a spear and sword and carrying a round shield and a helmet as armour.

304 Berserkers wore animal skins instead of armour. Some Viking warriors were known as 'berserkers', meaning 'bear-shirts', from their habit of wearing bear or wolf skins in battle.

◄ A Viking berserker attacks dressed in a bear skin. These warriors would fall into a terrible rage in battle and seemed to ignore all danger.

305
The battleaxe was a terrible weapon. Many Scandinavian peoples used a battleaxe that had a haft (handle) up to 2 metres long and a blade more than 30 centimetres across. It was used with both hands. In the hands of a master, it could kill a horse and rider with a single blow.

QUIZ
1. Which warriors wore animal skins?
2. Who won the Battle of Lechfeld?
3. Who built a dyke between England and Wales?

Answers:
1. Berserkers 2. The Germans 3. Offa

◄ A Viking raiding party wielding battleaxes attacks a group of Englishmen.

306
The heavy cavalrymen ruled the battlefield. In AD 955 a small army of German knights destroyed the larger Magyar cavalry at the Battle of Lechfeld, in Germany. Knights (mounted men in armour carrying a spear and sword) were recognized as the most effective type of soldier.

Early knights

307 The first knights wore mail armour. Around the year 1000, most body armour in Europe was made of mail. This was flexible to wear and could stop a sword blow with ease. Such armour was expensive to make so only richer men could afford to wear it.

1. Iron ring

2. Holes pierced in ends

3. Ends joined with a rivet

▲ Mail armour was made by linking together hundreds of small iron rings. The rings could be linked in a number of different ways, just like knitting a sweater.

308 Shields were decorated to identify their owners. From about 1150, knights wore helmets that covered their faces for extra protection. Around the same time, they began to paint heraldic designs (coats of arms) on their shields so that they could recognize each other in battle.

309 Early knights sometimes used leather armour. Mail armour was effective, but heavy and expensive, so some knights wore armour made of boiled, hardened leather. This was lighter and easier to wear, and was still some defence against attack.

◀ A knight in about 1100. He wears a shirt and trousers made of mail and a helmet shaped from a sheet of steel. His shield is made of wood.

310
Plate armour gave better protection than mail. By about 1300, new types of arrow and swords had developed to pierce mail armour. This led to the development of plate armour, made of sheets of steel shaped to fit the body, which arrows and swords could not easily penetrate.

311
The mace could smash armour to pieces. The most effective of the crushing weapons developed to destroy plate armour, the mace had a big metal head on a long shaft. A blow from a mace crushed plate armour, breaking the bones of the person wearing it.

The armour around the stomach and groin had to be flexible enough to allow bending and twisting movements

The most complicated section of plate armour was the gauntlet that covered the hands. It might contain 30 pieces of metal

The legs and feet were protected by armour that covered the limbs entirely

► A suit of plate armour made in Europe in the early 14th century.

QUIZ

1. Why did knights paint coats of arms on their shields?
2. How was leather armour treated to make it tough?
3. Which was the most effective crushing weapon?

Answers:
1. So that they could recognize each other in battle 2. It was boiled 3. The mace

Archers and peasants

312 **Infantry were usually poorly armed.** Around 1000 years ago, ordinary farmers or craftsmen would turn out to protect their homes against an enemy army. Such men could not afford armour and usually carried just a spear and a large knife or an axe. They usually guarded castles and towns.

▼ A Welsh spearman in about 1350. He carries a spear and sword, but has no armour at all.

◄ An English archer in about 1400. He wears a metal helmet and has quilted body armour.

313 **The longbow was a deadly weapon.** From about 1320 the English included thousands of archers in their armies. The archers were trained to shoot up to eight arrows each minute, producing a deadly rain of arrows that could slaughter an enemy force at a distance.

ARMS & ARMOUR

314 **Some weapons were based on farming tools.** Many soldiers used weapons that were simply specialized forms of farming tools. The bill was based on a hedge-trimmer but could be used to pull a knight from his horse, and then smash through his plate armour.

▲ The heads of an English bill (left) and Dutch godendag (right). Both were pole weapons used by infantrymen.

315 **Crossbows were used in some countries.** Soldiers from Italy, the Low Countries (now Belgium and the Netherlands) and some other areas of Europe preferred to use the crossbow instead of the bow. It could not shoot as quickly, but was easier to learn how to use and much more powerful.

316 **Some foot soldiers wore armour.** Infantrymen sent to war by wealthy towns or cities were often equipped with armour. They usually formed solid formations with their long spears pointing forward, and could be highly effective in battle.

◀ A crossbowman would hide behind a large shield called a pavise while reloading his weapon.

MAKE A CASTLE BOOKMARK

You will need:
card   scissors   crayons   sticky tape

1. Draw a tower 12 centimetres tall on card and cut it out.
2. Draw the top half of a soldier holding a shield on card and cut it out.
3. Colour in the tower and soldier.
4. Place the soldier so that his body is behind the tower and his shield in front.
5. Tape the soldier's body to the back of the tower to hold it in place.

Your bookmark is ready to use!

Later knights

317 Armoured knights were the most important troops. Knights had the best arms and armour and were the most experienced men in any army, so they were often put in command.

318 Knights sometimes fought on foot, instead of on horseback. English knights fought on foot after about 1300. This enabled them to hold a position more securely and co-operate more effectively with other soldiers.

▶ The bascinet helmet had a visor that could be lifted so the wearer could see and breathe.

I DON'T BELIEVE IT!

At the Battle of Agincourt in France in 1415, the English killed 10,000 Frenchmen, but only about 100 Englishmen lost their lives.

319 Horse armour made of metal and leather was introduced to protect horses. By about 1300, knights began to dress their horses in various sorts of armour. Horses without armour could be killed or injured by enemy arrows or spears, leaving the knight open to attack. Men with armoured horses were put in the front rank during battle.

▶ Horse armour was shaped to fit the horse's head and neck, then was left loose to dangle down over the legs.

320 The flail was a difficult weapon to use. It consisted of a big metal ball studded with spikes and attached to a chain on a wooden handle. It could inflict terrible injuries, but also swing back unexpectedly, so only men who practised with it for hours each day could use it properly.

◀ A knight uses a flail in foot combat.

321 Each man had his place in battle. Before each battle, the commander would position his men to ensure that the abilities of each were put to best use. The men with the best armour were placed where the enemy was expected to attack, while archers were positioned on the flank (left or right side) where they could shoot across the battlefield. Lightly armoured men were held in the rear, ready to chase enemy soldiers if they began to retreat.

Desert warfare

322
Bows were made of many materials. In the desert areas of the Middle East, soldiers used bows made from layers of animal horn, bone and sinew that were stuck tightly together and then carved into shape. These were called 'composite bows', and fired arrows with much greater force than longbows.

▲ The recurved bow was short, but powerful.

323
The Mongols wore light armour. A tribe from central Asia called the Mongols were led by Genghis Khan (1162–1227). Their armour was light because there was a lack of iron in Central Asia. As a result, they developed tactics based on fast-moving cavalry attacks.

324 **Curved swords were known as scimitars.** Armourers working in the city of Damascus, Syria, invented a new way to make swords around the year 1100. This involved folding the steel over on itself several times while the metal was white hot. The new type of steel was used to make curved swords that were both light in weight and incredibly sharp, called scimitars.

325 **Teneke armour was made up of a mail coat onto which were fixed overlapping pieces of flat metal.** These pieces were about 6 centimetres by 2 centimetres. The plates were loosely hinged so that air could pass through easily but blows from a sword could not. The armour was light, comfortable and effective, but it was also expensive.

▲ A Saracen wearing teneke armour and wielding a scimitar. The Saracens wore flowing cloaks and turbans to help combat the heat of the desert.

◀ A Mongol army attacks men from the city of Kiev, Ukraine. Although designed for grasslands and deserts, Mongol weaponry was effective in cold forests as well.

326 **Armour was light because of the desert heat.** The plate armour in use in Europe was not worn in the deserts of the Middle East. The plates of metal stopped air circulating around the body and were very uncomfortable to wear. Instead desert fighters in the 13th to 15th centuries wore loose robes and light pieces of armour.

Indian arms

▼ An Indian soldier who wears no armour, but carries a shield and a pata sword.

▶ Indian shields often had intricate designs to make them look more impressive.

327 India had a unique tradition of arms manufacture. Between 1650 and 1800 the vast lands south of the Himalayas, modern India, Pakistan and Bangladesh, were divided into lots of small states. Each state had its own army, and made great efforts to have impressive weapons.

328 The khanda was a sword with a long, straight blade. These swords had heavy, double-edged blades that often had handles big enough to allow them to be held in both hands. Larger khanda were slung from a belt over the shoulder so that they hung down the user's back.

329 Indian soldiers used the pata. This was an iron glove (gauntlet) that extended almost to the elbow, attached to a sword blade. It was very useful for thrusting, especially when attacking infantry from horseback, but was less effective at cutting.

330 Talwars were curved swords with a single, sharp cutting edge. The handles were often rounded, rather like the butt of a pistol. They were highly decorated with silver, gold and semi-precious stones.

▲ The talwar sword was invented around AD 1000 and was used in battle for over 900 years.

331 Elephants were used in warfare. A small platform, ('howdah'), was strapped to the back of the elephant. Men armed with bows, or later with guns, sat in the howdah and shot at the enemy over the elephant's head.

► War elephants were often covered in armour, while the howdah, in which the soldiers sat, could be covered with iron.

Island wars

332 Polynesians fought without armour or shields. The islands in the Pacific Ocean were home to people of the Polynesian culture. Before contact with Europeans around 1750, the Polynesians made their weapons from natural materials. They preferred to rely on skill and movement in battle rather than armour, though some men wore thick shirts of plaited coconut fibres as protection.

333 Shark teeth were made into swords. In western Polynesia, shark teeth were added to the sides of long clubs to produce a weapon called the tebutje. This was used to cut as well as smash and was a vicious close-combat weapon.

▼ A Polynesian war canoe on its way to a raid on another island. The warriors paddling the canoe kept their weapons beside them.

▲ Boomerangs often had decorative carvings or were brightly painted.

335 War clubs were favoured weapons.

Wooden clubs were carved from single pieces of wood and were over one metre in length. They had wide, heavy heads that were often elaborately carved with shapes and patterns.

► A Maori mere, or short club. These weapons were made from very hard woods.

334 The boomerang didn't always come back.

Native Australian people used spears and bows and arrows, as well as the boomerang. This heavy throwing stick was shaped so that it spun round in the air and could be thrown with accuracy. Only the lighter boomerangs, used for hunting birds, were designed to come back to the thrower.

336 The Maori used wooden weapons.

The Polynesian people who live in New Zealand are known as the Maori. They produced unique types of club. One type was the mere, which had a short handle and a wide curved blade that could be used for slashing at the enemy.

I DON'T BELIEVE IT!

In the Fiji islands warriors would often use a wooden club shaped like a pineapple to attack their victims.

African arms

337 **The iklwa was a deadly weapon.** The Zulu nation of southern Africa was ruled by King Shaka from 1816–1828, who built up an empire covering thousands of square kilometres. Shaka introduced a new weapon, the iklwa, a short spear with a broad blade used for stabbing. It proved more deadly than the traditional throwing spears used by other peoples in the area.

338 **Assegai were throwing spears.** They had smaller and lighter heads than the iklwa. Zulu warriors would begin a battle by throwing their two or three assegai. Then they would run quickly forward to attack with their iklwa.

339 **Helmets were for show, not defence.** Zulu warriors wore headdresses to make them look tall and impressive. They were made of wickerwork with tall ostrich feathers, flowing crane feathers and strips of coloured fur or woollen tufts attached.

340 Knobkerries could crush skulls.

Many Zulu warriors carried a heavy wooden club, or knobkerrie, as well as the iklwa. If the iklwa was lost, the knobkerrie could be used for close fighting.

341 Shields were made of cowhide.

Zulu shields were nearly 2 metres in length, and were cut from cowhide, which was laced onto a central wooden pole with strips of leather.

MAKE ZULU PUPPETS

You will need:
card   ice-lolly sticks
crayons   glue

1. Draw some Zulu warriors onto card.
2. Cut out each of the warriors and colour them in.
3. Glue an ice-lolly stick to the back of each warrior.
4. If you make enough Zulus, glue the lolly sticks to a straight piece of wood so that the warriors form a rank.

◄ A Zulu impi, or army, on the march. Boys followed the warriors carrying bedding, food and spare weapons.

The Americas

342 In South America, spears were thrown at the start of a battle. The Aztec people built up a large empire in what is now Mexico between 1400 and 1510. Their warriors won a series of battles against other American peoples. Each battle began with men on both sides throwing light javelins at the enemy. Then the men would charge at each other to fight at close quarters.

◄ In battle, some Aztec warriors dressed as eagles, jaguars and other fierce animals.

343 Obsidian stone was razor sharp. The Aztec, Maya and other peoples of South America did not know how to make iron or bronze, so they made their weapons from natural materials. The most effective weapons were edged with slivers of obsidian, a hard, glasslike stone that has a very sharp edge when first broken.

344
Clubs were used to knock enemies unconscious. One of the main purposes of warfare among the Maya and Aztec people was to capture prisoners. The prisoners were then taken to temples to be sacrificed to gods such as Huitzilopochtli, the god of war, by having their hearts cut out while still beating.

345
Shields were highly decorated. The shields used by Aztec and Maya warriors were made of wood, and covered with brightly coloured animal skins and feathers. They often had strings of feathers or fur dangling down underneath to deflect javelins.

◀ The Maya tried to capture enemy noblemen and rulers to use as sacrifices to the gods.

346
The tomahawk was a famous weapon of the North American tribes. This was a short-handled axe with a heavy head. The first tomahawks were made with stone heads, but after Europeans reached North America, the tribes began buying steel-headed tomahawks.

▶ The native peoples of the eastern areas of North America used spears and special axes, known as tomahawks.

The end of an era

◄ A wheel–lock pistol from about 1650. The wheel–lock was the first reliable firing mechanism.

347 **The first guns could not penetrate heavy armour.** Early forms of gunpowder were not powerful enough to shoot a bullet from a hand-held gun with much force. By 1600, armourers were producing helmets and breastplates that were bulletproof.

349 **Cavalry continued to wear body armour.** Until 1914, cavalry engaged in fast-moving fights could often not reload their guns once they had been fired. As a result cavalrymen often fought using swords and lances, so armour was still useful.

348 **Cannons could destroy armour.** Large cannons fired iron or stone balls that weighed up to 25 kilograms. They were designed to knock down stone walls, but were also used in battle. No armour could survive being hit by such a weapon.

◄ A musketeer in about 1660. Each cartridge on his belt holds a bullet and powder to fire it.

▼ A French cavalryman in 1810. He wears an iron helmet and iron body armour.

350
Infantry officers wore gorget armour. This was one of the last kinds of armour to be worn. It was a small piece of armour that fitted under the front of the helmet and protected the neck. Gorgets were often used to show the rank of the man wearing them, so they continued to be worn long after helmets were abandoned. They were used until 1914 in some countries.

▶ A musketeer in about 1770. He is using a ramrod to push the bullet and gunpowder down the barrel of a gun before firing it.

351
By 1850 most soldiers no longer wore armour. As guns became more effective, they were able to fire bullets with greater accuracy over longer distances and with more power. By 1850 most infantry were armed with guns that could shoot through any type of armour, so most soldiers stopped wearing armour.

I DON'T BELIEVE IT!

As late as 1914 some French cavalry went to war wearing armour, despite the fact that they had to face artillery and machine guns.

Modern arms and armour

352 The first modern use of chemical weapons was in World War I. In April 1915, the Germans used poison gas against French soldiers. It worked by irritating the lining of the lungs and throat. Soldiers then began to wear anti-gas uniforms as protection.

▶ A British infantryman in 1944. He wears a steel helmet and carries a Sten gun – a light machine gun.

▲ A British cavalryman charges in 1916. Both the man and horse wear gasmasks to protect them against poison gas.

353 Modern soldiers always wear helmets. Exploding shells and rockets often throw out sharp splinters of metal called shrapnel. Soldiers take cover in trenches or holes. Metal helmets protect the head, the most likely part of the body to be hit by shrapnel.

▶ A Main Battle Tank (MBT) advances through the desert. The arrival of tanks and other armoured vehicles has transformed modern warfare.

354 Modern armoured warfare involves tanks.

The armour needed to stop modern shells and rockets is too heavy for a person to carry, but it can be mounted on a vehicle, such as a tank or an armoured personnel carrier (APC). These vehicles are the key feature of a modern army, as the armoured knights were in the middle ages.

355 The best armour makes you disappear.

Camouflage conceals soldiers by using colours that blend into the background of plants, sky or sand. Helmets often have a strap that can be used to attach vegetation for extra camouflage.

356 Bomb disposal soldiers use special armour.

Designed to give protection against blast waves, the armour covers as much of the body as possible while still allowing the soldier to use his hands to defuse the bomb.

▼ An American soldier in Iraq. He wears bulletproof body armour as well as a helmet.

Index

Entries in **bold** refer to main subject entries. Entries in *italics* refer to illustrations.

Acknowledgements

The publishers would like to thank the following sources for the use of their photographs:
Key: t = top, b = bottom, l = left, r = right, c = centre, bg = background, rt = repeated throughout

Front cover illustration Stuart Jackson Carter

Endpapers Tomasz Bidermann/ShutterstockPremier

Alamy 44(b) John Muggenborg; 81(b) Mary Evans Picture Library; 86(b) United Archives GmbH; 89(b) & 91(b) JTB Media Creation, Inc.; 93(b) V&A Images; 105(b) Interofoto; 112–113(b) Photos 12; 118(bc) Tibor Bognar/Alamy Stock Photo

Fotolia 45(tl) Roy; 104(b) Kirsty Pargeter; 105(b) pdtnc; 117(tr) U.P.images;

Getty 14–15(bg) Bryna Productions/Universal Pictures/Bettman; 88(b) John Stevenson; 91(b) John Stevenson; 92(b) John Stevenson; 106(b) Tom Grill/Corbis/Fuse; 114–115(b) Hiroshi Higuchi; 116(tl) De Agostini Picture Library

Movie Store Collection 119(b) Warner Bros./Bedford Falls Company, Cruise/Wagner Productions

Pictorial Press 43(b) Dreamworks/Universal Pictures/Scott Free Productions; 45(br) Bryna Productions, Inc./Universal Pictures; 46(tl) Dreamworks/Universal Pictures/Scott Free Productions

ShutterstockPremier 1 Panos Karas; 2–3 ESOlex; 16(tr) Andrei Nekrassov; 83(b) The Art Archive/Gianni Dagli Orti/Rex; 95(b) The Art Archive/ Bibliothèque des Arts Décoratifs Paris/Gianni Dagli Orti/Rex; 99(b) The Art Archive/Rex; 100–101(b) Art Archive/Gunshots/Rex; 101(b) Rex/ The Art Archive/Gunshots; 116–117(bg) The Art Archive/British Museum/Rex

Topfoto 6–7(bg) J. Balean; 42(tr) ©2006 Alinari; 117(tr) Print Collector/HIP

All other photographs are from: DigitalSTOCK, digitalvision, John Foxx, PhotoAlto, PhotoDisc, PhotoEssentials, PhotoPro, Stockbyte

All artworks are from the Miles Kelly Artwork Bank

Every effort has been made to acknowledge the source and copyright holder of each picture.
Miles Kelly Publishing apologizes for any unintentional errors or omissions.